GOOD HOUSEKEEPING

TRADITIONAL
KNITTING

GOOD HOUSEKEEPING
TRADITIONAL KNITTING

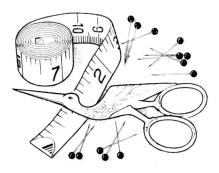

EBURY PRESS

Editor
Amy Carroll

Assistant Editor
Melanie Miller

Designer
Derek Coombes

Good Housekeeping Traditional Knitting
was conceived, edited and designed by
Dorling Kindersley Limited, 9 Henrietta Street, London WC2E 8PS

First published in Great Britain in 1983 by
Ebury Press
Division of the National Magazine Company Limited
Colquhoun House
27-37 Broadwick Street
London W1V 1FR

Second impression 1986

ISBN 0 85223 277 2

Printed in Singapore

Contents

Introduction

The urge to decorate our apparel is a characteristic
shared by all cultures, and is also one of the prime
ways in which we discriminate among them. The origins of
knitting are still unproven, but that it has been in
existence for a very long time is nowhere in doubt.

Design was integral to even the earliest cultures and
through the use of symbolic patterns, people tried to
come to terms with the life they lived. Therefore, they
knitted into their garments animals, plants and features
in the landscape, as well as their activities, tokens
of affection and spiritual longings.

The differing physical characteristics of the land as well
as the various employments of people on it, have resulted
in great diversity in patterns from around the world.
The seafaring British Isles are known for their warm and
decorative fishermen's sweaters and women's lacy scarfs; South
American patterns are often graphic representations of their
native creatures – both real and fantastic; Scandinavian motifs
employ the snowflake, fir tree and reindeer; Europe translates its
myriad flora and fauna into highly decorative patterns, while
Asia contributes lacy evocations of its sacred symbols.

Today's knitters have several advantages over earlier
craftspeople. They do not have to follow the traditional
uses of specific patterns, after all, Aran patterns look
very effective on furnishings. Also, there is an enormous
range of yarns in which the wide variety of patterns from all
over the world can be interpreted. Use the patterns inside
on your favourite garment shapes or create new ones to display
them; by doing so you'll be wearing something that has survived
the test of centuries.

BASIC TECHNIQUES

NEEDLES

Knitting needles are machine-made from plastic-coated light-weight aluminium, steel, plastic or wood. You can buy pairs of needles with knobs at one end for knitting back and forth in rows; double-pointed needles, in sets of three or more, and circular needles for knitting "in the round"; short cable needles for holding stitches in twisted cable patterns. All needles are graded in different sizes according to their diameter, from 2mm to 25mm. Buy good quality needles with well-shaped points.

YARNS

In addition to wool and the many synthetic yarns now produced, you can knit with cotton, string, ribbon, rafia or any pliable fibre.

Fibres used to produce hand-knitting yarns generally fall into two main categories–natural and man-made – while many commercial yarns are classified according to their construction, eg. 3-4-ply and crêpe.

Ply Fibres are first spun into single threads, called a ply, and then the threads are twisted together to make a specific yarn. Note that "ply" does not indicate a standard thickness of thread, but refers directly to the number of single threads used in making a specific yarn.

Which yarn? It is essential to choose the most appropriate yarn and stitch pattern to suit your specific needs. Generally, firm, windproof fabrics are produced with thick yarn and relatively small needles; soft, yet thick and warm fabrics require lightly twisted middle-weight yarn and bigger needles, while baby wear demands soft, washable yarn and small needles.

2-3 ply wool

baby wool quick knit

4-ply botany

Shetland

double knitting

double double knitting

chunky

synthetic crêpe

wool crêpe

double crêpe

mohair

angora

novelty tweed

bouclé

poodle

knitting cottons

chenille

cotton slub

lurex

metallic mix

7

CASTING ON

All hand knitting starts with a number of loops being cast on to one needle and further rows are then worked into these loops.

1 *Make a slip loop on LH needle. Insert RH needle through loop from front to back.*

2 *Bring working yarn under and over the RH needle.*

3 *Draw loop through slip stitch and transfer to LH needle. Repeat steps 1 and 2.*

BASIC KNIT STITCH

1 *With yarn at back, insert RH needle from front to back into first stitch on LH needle.*

2 *Bring working yarn under and over the RH needle point.*

3 *Draw loop through, discarding worked stitch on LH needle. Continue in this way to end of row.*

Complete the first row and turn the work around. Take the needle carrying the stitches into the left hand and the empty needle in the right. With back of work now facing, begin a new row.

BASIC PURL STITCH

1 *With yarn at front, insert RH needle from back to front into first stitch on LH needle.*

2 *Bring working yarn over and around RH needle point.*

3 *Draw loop through, discarding worked stitch on LH needle. Continue in this way to end of row.*

Changing from a knit stitch
to a purl stitch (eg. "ribbing"); k3, bring yarn to front of work, p3.

Changing from a purl stitch
to a knit stitch (eg. "ribbing"); p3, take yarn to back of work, k3.

CASTING OFF

Secure the stitches of your finished piece of knitting by casting off. This is usually done on a knit row but the same method is used when purling. For casting off in rib, remember to position your yarn correctly before knitting or purling the two working stitches.

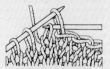  

To cast off k-wise
1 *Knit first 2 stitches and insert point of LH needle into first st.*

2 *Lift first stitch over second and off needle. K1 stitch and continue to lift one stitch over another to end of row.*

To cast off p-wise
Purl first 2 stitches and continue as for knit row.

SELVEDGES AND SEAMS

  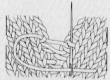

Open selvedge
(use on unseamed edges) Slip first and last sts on every k row knitwise. Purl all sts in p row.

Slip stitch selvedge
(use on seamed edges) Slip first st purlwise and knit last st on every row.

Invisible seam *With RS facing, pick up 1 st and pull yarn through. Pick up next st from opposite side; repeat.*

INCREASING

"Invisible" increasing doesn't leave a hole in the knitted fabric and is generally used in the construction of garments. Use **(inc 1)** method mainly for shaping side edges and **(M1, k up 1, or p up 1)** for tailored shaping made within the body of the knitting.

Inc 1 k
K into front of stitch but before discarding loop, k into back.

Inc 1 p
P into front of stitch but before discarding loop, p into back.

Completed increase
2 stitches from 1; purlwise on left, knitwise on right.

M1 k-wise
1 *Insert LH needle under running thread between 2 stitches.*

2 *Knit into back of raised loop, twisting it so as not to leave a hole in the fabric.*

3 *Invisible M1 (left)* For **visible variation** *(right) knit into front of running thread.*

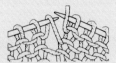

M1 p-wise
1 *Insert LH needle under running thread between 2 stitches.*

2 *Purl into back of raised loop, twisting it so as not to leave a hole in the fabric.*

3 *Invisible M1 (left)* For **visible variation** *(right) purl into front of running thread.*

Knit up one (k up 1) is often referred to as a "lifted increase" since it picks up the loop of stitch below next to be worked; it is barely visible in the finished fabric.

1 *With RH needle knit into top of st below next one to be worked.*

2 *Knit next stitch on LH needle; continue to end of row.*

Purl up one (p up 1) is a "lifted increase" made by purling into top loop of stitch in row below. As in k up 1, the new stitch is made on the RH needle.

1 *With RH needle purl into top of st below next one to be worked.*

2 *Purl next stitch on LH needle; continue to end of row.*

DECORATIVE INCREASING

This method of increasing forms eyelet holes in the fabric and may be used not only for practical purposes, such as buttonholes, or to highlight a raglan seam, but mainly as the basis for all lace knitting. Work lace patterns by increasing stitches, using either (**yfwd/yo**) or (**yrn**) method, and decreasing in the same row in order to compensate for the made stitches.

Yfwd/yo
1 *Bring yarn forward, loop it over RH needle and knit next stitch.*

2 *With loop and stitch transferred to your RH needle, continue to end of row.*

3 *On following row, purl into loop in the usual way. Work in pattern to end of row.*

Yrn
1 *Take yarn round RH needle to front of work. Purl next stitch.*

2 *With loop and stitch transferred to your RH needle, continue to end of row.*

3 *On following row, knit into loop in the usual way. Work in pattern to end of row.*

DECREASING

The simplest way to decrease is to knit or purl 2 stitches together (**k2 tog/p2 tog**) at either end of the row or at any given point. To make a special feature of decreasing, use the slip stitch method where the decreases are worked in pairs, one slanting to the left and the other to the right, as on a raglan sleeve.

K2tog
Insert RH needle through 2 sts and k tog as 1 st. Dec slants L to R.

P2tog
Insert RH needle through 2 sts and p tog as 1 st. Dec slants L to R.

P/K2tog tbl
Purl or knit 2 stitches together through back of loop, for decrease to slant R to L.

Slip stitch dec (k) (sl 1, k1, psso)
1 *Slip next st from LH needle onto RH needle.*

2 *Hold slipped stitch and knit next stitch in usual way.*

3 *Using point of LH needle, lift slipped stitch over knit stitch and off RH needle. Dec slants R to L.*

Slip stitch dec (p) (sl 1, p1, psso)
1 *Slip next stitch from LH needle onto RH needle.*

2 *Hold slipped stitch and purl next stitch in usual way.*

3 *Using point of LH needle, lift slipped stitch over purl stitch and off RH needle. Dec slants L to R on RS.*

MAKING A CHAIN EYELET (k2, yo, k2tog)

Prevent uneven selvedges by starting eyelet patterns 2 sts in from beginning of row and finishing 2 sts from end. To keep number of sts in repeat constant, increases and decreases should be equal.

1 *Knit 2 stitches, yarn over, knit 2 together.*

2 *Yarn over stitch replaces knit 2 together.*

3 *Detail of finished chain eyelet.*

11

USING A CABLE NEEDLE (cn)

For twisting 2 or more stitches, a double-pointed cable needle should be used. The stitches to be twisted are slipped onto it and held, either at the front or back of the work, until ready to be knitted. Stitches held at the front will twist cable from right to left while those held at the back will twist cable from left to right.

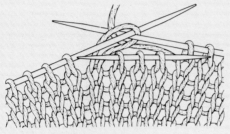

To twist a six stitch cable, slip first 3 sts onto cn and hold at front of work. Knit next 3 sts, then knit first 3 sts off cn.

Completed cable twist from right to left.

ADDING NEW COLOURS

Add a new ball of yarn or another colour, as in horizontal stripes at the beginning of a row; the yarn is either broken off or carried up the side of the work until it is needed. For more intricate colourwork, eg. "jacquard", new yarn may be introduced at the beginning or in the middle of a row. Darn all loose ends neatly into the selvedge or through back of work.

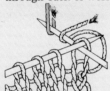

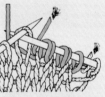

Beginning new row
1 *Insert RH needle into 1st stitch on LH needle. K 1 st using old and new yarns tog.*

2 Leave old yarn at the back and knit next 2 stitches with 2 strands of new yarn.

3 Discard short end of new yarn and continue to knit. Pick up old yarn from side edge if required later.

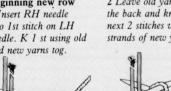

Middle of row
1 *Insert RH needle into next st on LH needle. Wrap new yarn over RH needle, k st.*

2 Leave old yarn at the back and knit next 2 stitches with 2 strands of new yarn.

3 Discard short end of new yarn and continue to knit. Use new and old yarns as required in pattern.

STRANDING YARN

Use the stranding method for working narrow stripes, small dot or check repeats, and for traditional Fair Isle patterns with 2 colours in a row. Strand yarn over 2 to 5 stitches but weave in over 5, keeping an even tension throughout.

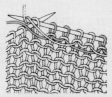

RS row cols A, B
With A, k2, leave at back. Carry B loosely across back, k2.
On a p row, *carry yarn across front.*

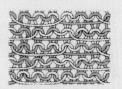

For correct tension, *take care not to pull loose stranding yarn too tight on WS.*

WEAVING YARN

Use weaving technique for carrying coloured yarns over more than 5 sts. This will avoid making long, unsightly strands of yarn which can catch and distort the fabric. Remember, stranding and weaving will produce double thickness.

RS row cols A, B
1. With both yarns at back, B in LH and A in RH, k1. On 2nd and alt sts insert needle and bring B in LH over A.

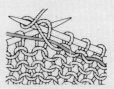

2. With A, complete k st keeping B below A.
On a p row *weave yarns in same way carrying them at front of work.*

COLOURSLIP

These intricate-looking patterns have a simple working method based on combining 2-colour horizontal stripes with slip stitches. Only 1 colour at a time is knitted. Carry any yarns not in use up side of work.

RS row: *With 2nd colour yarn at back, slip next stitch p-wise off LH needle.*

WS row: *Carrying 2nd colour yarn loosely across front, p next st in usual way.*

CROSSING YARN

Work large blocks of colour, eg. diagonal or wide vertical stripes or jacquard motifs, with separate bobbins of yarn for each colour repeated in a row, twisting them on WS as colour change is made.

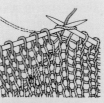

Diagonal stripe
L to R: *Cross 1st col in front of 2nd; pick up 2nd, k.*
P row: *colours encroach.*

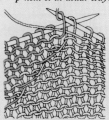

Diagonal stripe
R to L: *Cross 1st colour behind 2nd; pick up 2nd and p.*
K row: *colours encroach.*

13

PUTTING THE STITCH PATTERNS TO USE

Before you begin to knit any item you should always work a tension sample first. This is necessary whether you intend to use a printed pattern; substitute the given stitch and/or yarn, with another; or, use your own design.

TENSION

Tension involves the relationship between yarn and needles and the way your fingers control the yarn. With practice you will notice, for example, that thicker yarns require a slacker control of tension while thinner yarns require a tighter control. Any tension variation within a garment will give an uneven appearance. By calculating stitches and rows, your tension sample will also show whether the yarn and needles you are using will make up into the size, shape and weight you require. Printed patterns give a tension guide stating the number of stitches and rows to a 10cm square using the recommended yarn and needles.

To make a tension sample, begin by working a square slightly larger than 10cm. Place it on a flat surface and, using pins, mark out the tension measurement given in the pattern.

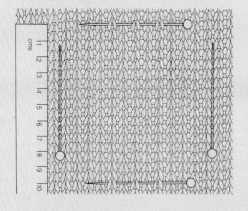

Count the rows and stitches between the pins and if they are the same as in the pattern, then your tension is correct. If there are too many stitches between pins, then your tension is too tight and you should try one, or more size larger needles. Too few stitches, and you should try one, or more, size smaller.

SUBSTITUTING ONE STITCH FOR ANOTHER

This opens up many new design opportunities providing that the stitch you substitute is of a similiar type to the original one given in the pattern, and that the "multiple of stitches" will fit. Patterns combining different stitches within a row require a specific number or multiple of stitches so that the pattern repeats evenly across a row. For instance, a particular pattern may call for a multiple of 8 stitches plus 2. You should then cast on 8, 16, 24, 32 sts or more according to your required width, plus 2 sts, which go at either end of the row, to be used for the seams. Using the recommended yarn, work a tension sample in the new stitch, and at the same time, calculate the multiple of stitches and adjust if necessary. With small multiples it may be possible to equally divide any left-over stitches to the side edges. You

14

may also substitute one yarn for another, providing you follow the same principle of chooosing one from the same category as the original, eg. 4-ply or mohair, and working a tension sample first.

DESIGNING WITH A TENSION GRID

For your first attempt at designing a knitted garment, one of the best methods is to use the tension grid technique to establish how many stitches are required for pattern and shape (see pp9, 11 for increasing and decreasing). Begin with a simple stitch pattern and with yarn and needles of your choice, work a tension sample, counting the exact number of rows and stitches.

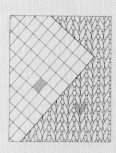 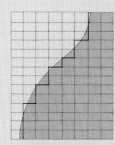

To get an accurate outline of the shape, draw on a large sheet of tracing paper a grid to match the size of your tension stitch. Note that the knitted stitch is usually rectangular. Place paper pattern under grid, trace off outline, stepping curves to match grid lines.

You will now see from your grid exactly how many stitches you will need to cast on and precisely where to make increases and decreases for shaping. Economize by using the same grid for further pattern components by over-tracing in contrasting colours.

ESTIMATING YARN QUANTITIES

If you intend using a spinner's yarn, a reliable method of estimating quantity is to take a printed pattern of the same style and use the suggested quantities as a guide. Another method is to knit a ball of yarn in your chosen stitch, measure the area, then estimate the total area of your design and calculate how much it will take to complete it.

NEEDLE AND YARN TABLE

2mm	2-ply, 3-ply, baby yarn	5	double, double knitting
2¼		5½	
2¾		6	
2¾	4-ply, baby quick-knits	6½	chunky yarn, mohair
3		7	
3¼		7½	
3¼	double knitting	8	heavyweight yarns
3¾		9	
4		10	
4½			

ABBREVIATIONS

alt	alternately	patt	pattern
BC	back cross	psso	pass slipped stitch over
beg	beginning	p2sso	pass 2 slipped stitches over
BKC	back knit cross	p up	pick up and purl
col	colour	p-wise	purlwise
cont	continu(e/ing)	R	right
cn	cable needle	rem	remain(ing)
dec	decreas(e/ing)	rep	repeat
dpn	double-pointed needle	RH	right-hand
DL	drop loop	RN	right needle
FC	front cross	RS	right side
FKC	front knit cross	RT	right twist
foll	following	SBC	single back cross
g st	garter stitch	SFC	single front cross
inc	increas(e/ing)	sl	slip
k	knit	sl st	slip stitch
k up	pick up and knit	st(s)	stitches
k1-b	knit one into back	st st	stocking stitch
k-wise	knitwise	tbl	through back of loop(s)
L	left	tog	together
LH	left-hand	WS	wrong side
LN	left needle	wyib	with yarn in back
LT	left twist	wyif	with yarn in front
M1	make one	ybk	yarn back
MB	make bobble	yfwd/yo	yarn forward/yarn over
m-st	moss stitch	yon	yarn over needle
no(s)	number(s)	yrn	yarn round needle
p	purl	y2rn	yarn twice round needle

Symbols
A star * shown in a pattern row denotes that the stitches shown after this sign must be repeated from that point.
Round brackets ( ), enclosing a particular stitch combination, denote that the stitch combination must be repeated in the order shown.

FRUIT & FLOWERS

Inspiration for decorative patterns in Europe came largely from native plants – wherein the fruit was prized as much as the flower. Life on the land was often translated into richly patterned handknit fabrics which were created as less expensive alternatives to the fashionable brocades.

Daisy stitch

Materials Medium-weight wool or synthetic mixes for a pretty, decorative effect.

Uses All-over pattern for girl's or woman's cardigan, baby's bonnet and jacket set, or blanket.

Multiple of 4 sts plus 1.

Rows 1 and 3 (RS) Knit.
Row 2 K1, *p3tog, yo (wrapping yarn completely around needle), purl same 3 sts tog again, k1; rep from *.

Row 4 K1, p1, k1, *p3tog, yo, purl same 3 sts tog again, k1; rep from *, end p1, k1.
Repeat rows 1 to 4.

Strawberries

Materials Angora, mohair or lightweight yarn for garments; crochet cotton for furnishings.

Uses All-over pattern for bed-jacket, child's dress or sweater set; border for apron, buffet runner or tray cloth.

Multiple of 12 sts plus 1.

Row 1 (RS) Sl 1, k1, psso, *k4, yo, k1, yo, k4, sl 1, k2tog, psso; rep from *, end last repeat sl 1, k1, psso, instead of sl 1, k2tog, psso.

Row 2 P2tog, *(p3, yo) twice, p3, p3tog; rep from *, end last repeat p2tog instead of p3tog.

Row 3 Sl 1, k1, psso, *k2, yo, k5, yo, k2, sl 1, k2tog, psso; rep from *, end last repeat sl 1, k1, psso instead of sl 1, k2tog, psso.

Row 4 P2tog, *p1, yo, p7, yo, p1, p3tog; rep from *, end last repeat p2tog instead of p3tog.

Row 5 Sl 1, k1, psso, *yo, k9, yo, sl 1, k2tog, psso; rep from *, end last

repeat sl 1, k1, psso, instead of sl 1, k2tog, psso.

Row 6 P1, *yo, p4, p3tog, p4, yo, p1; rep from *.

Row 7 K2, *yo, k3, sl 1, k2tog, psso, k3, yo, k3; rep from *, end last repeat k2.

Row 8 P3, *yo, p2, p3tog, p2, yo, p5; rep from *, end last repeat p3.

Row 9 K4, *yo, k1, sl 1, k2tog, psso, k1, yo, k7; rep from *, end last repeat k4.

Row 10 P5, *yo, p3tog, yo, p9; rep from *, end last repeat p5.

Repeat rows 1 to 10.

Flower garden

Materials Medium-weight wool, or textured silk and cotton.
Uses Horizontal band for skirt border; inset panel for child's dress.

Multiple of 12 sts plus 1.

Rows 1, 3, and 5 (RS) P12, *k1-b, p11; rep from *, end p1.

Rows 2, 4, 6 and 8 K12, *p1-b, k11; rep from *, end k1.

Row 7 P8, *insert a crochet hook from front through fabric at right of twisted knit st in first row, catch yarn and draw through a long, loose loop, sl this loop onto right needle, knit next st and pass loop over st, p3, k1-b, p3, draw through another loop from left of same st in first row, sl loop onto right needle, knit next st and pass loop over it, p3; rep from *, end p5.

Row 9 P12, *(k1, yo) 3 times and k1, all in same st, making 7 sts from one, p11; rep from *, end p1.

Row 10 K12, *p7, k11; rep from *, end k1.

Row 11 P12, *k2tog-b, k3tog-b, k2tog, p11; rep from *, end p1.

Row 12 K12, *p3tog, k11; rep from *, end k1.

Rows 13, 15, and 17 P6, *k1-b, p11; rep from *, end last repeat p6.

Rows 14, 16, 18, and 20 K6, *p1-b, k11; rep from *, end last repeat k6.

Row 19 P2, *draw through a long loop from right of twisted knit st in row 13 and pass loop over next st as before, p3, k1-b, p3, draw through another loop from left of same st and pass loop over next st as before, p3; rep from *, end last repeat p2.

Row 21 P6, *make 7 sts from 1 as before, p11; rep from *, end last repeat p6.

Row 22 K6, *p7, k11; rep from *, end last repeat k6.

Row 23 P6, *k2tog-b, k3tog-b, k2tog, p11; rep from *, end last repeat p6.

Row 24 K6, *p3tog, k11; rep from *, end last repeat k6.

Repeat rows 1 to 24.

Wheat ear cable

Materials Double knitting or Aran-type yarn for sculptured look; medium-weight yarn for a deep-textured fabric.
Uses Inset panel for sleeveless pullover, cardigan, socks or gloves; all-over pattern for cushion cover or bedspread.

Panel of 17 sts.

Row 1 (RS) P2, k13, p2.
Row 2 K2, p13, k2.
Row 3 P2, sl next 3 sts to cn and hold at back, k3, k3 from cn, k1, sl next 3 sts to cn and hold at front, k3, k3 from cn, p2.
Row 4 K2, p13, k2.
Repeat rows 1 to 4.

Wheat Ear
Cable

Reverse
Wheat Ear
Cable

Reverse Wheat Ear Cable

Materials As above.
Uses As above.

Panel of 17 sts.

Row 1 (RS) P2, k13, p2.
Row 2 K2, p13, k2.
Row 3 P2, sl next 3 sts to cn and hold at front, k3, k3 from cn, k1, sl next 3 sts to cn and hold at back, k3, k3 from cn, p2.
Row 4 K2, p13, k2.
Repeat rows 1 to 4.

Grain of wheat

Materials Lurex mix or flecked wool for glittery effect; light-weight yarn for day wear.

Uses All-over pattern for evening jacket, baby's blanket or sleeping bag.

Multiple of 4 sts.

Note *Left Twist (LT): miss one st and knit into back of second st. Knit the missed st, then slip both sts from needle together.*

Right Twist (RT): miss one st and knit into front of second st. Knit the missed st, then slip both sts from needle together.

Row 1 (WS) Purl.

Row 2 K1, p2, *LT, p2; rep from *, end k1.

Row 3 K3, *p2, k2; rep from *, end k1.

Row 4 K3, *RT, k2; rep from *, end k1.

Row 5 Purl.

Row 6 K1, *LT, p2; rep from *, end LT, k1.

Row 7 K1, p2, *k2, p2; rep from *, end k1.

Row 8 K1, *RT, k2; rep from *, end RT, k1.

Repeat rows 1 to 8.

Corn on the cob

Materials Double knitting yarn or heavy-weight cotton for a warm, dense effect.

Uses All-over pattern for winter-weight coats and jackets, pram covers, blankets or throws.

Even number of sts.

Yarns A and B.
Cast on with A and knit one row.
Row 1 (RS) With B, k1, *k1, sl 1 wyib; rep from *, end k1.
Row 2 With B, k1, *sl 1 wyif, k1; rep from *, end k1.

Row 3 With A, k1, *sl 1 wyib, k1-b; rep from *, end k1.
Row 4 With A, k1, *k1, sl 1 wyif; rep from *, end k1.
Repeat rows 1 to 4.

Berry in a box

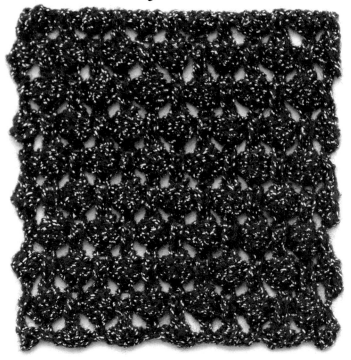

Materials Metallic, slubbed, crinkled, or ombré yarn, or lightweight chenille for a decorative look.

Uses All-over pattern for evening sweater or jacket; inset panel for dress yoke.

Multiple of 6 sts plus 1.

Row 1 (RS) P3, *k1, p5; rep from *, end k1, p3.

Row 2 K3tog, *yo, (k1, yo, k1) in next st, yo, decrease 5 as follows: k2tog-b, k3tog, pass the k2tog-b st over the k3tog st; rep from *, end yo, (k1, yo, k1) in next st, yo, k3tog-b.

Rows 3 and 5 K1, *p5, k1; rep from *.

Row 4 P1, *k5, p1; rep from *.

Row 6 Inc in first st, *yo, decrease 5 as in row 2, yo, (k1, yo, k1) in next st; rep from *, end yo, decrease 5, yo, inc in last st.

Row 7 As row 1.

Row 8 K3, *p1, k5; rep from *, end p1, k3.

Repeat rows 1 to 8.

Anemones

Materials Heavyweight or chunky yarn in cotton or wool for furnishings; double knitting for garments.

Uses All-over pattern for afghans, blankets or cushion covers; or winter-weight jackets or coats.

Multiple of 4 sts.

Note *For the two colour version work rows 1 and 2 in one colour, rows 3 and 4 in another.*

Row 1 (WS) Purl, wrapping yarn twice for each st.

Row 2 *Sl 4 sts briefly in order to drop extra wraps, replace the 4 elongated sts on left needle, then (k4tog, p4tog) twice into these same 4 sts; rep from *.

Row 3 P2, purl across wrapping yarn twice for each st, to the last 2 sts, end p2.

Row 4 K2; rep from * of row 2 across to the last 2 sts, end k2.

Repeat rows 1 to 4.

Cactus flower

Materials Medium-weight yarn for a rich-textured fabric; lurex, rayon or silk mix for a sparkling effect.

Uses All-over pattern for toddler's jacket and matching hat; inset panel for evening waistcoat, belt or purse.

Multiple of 6 sts plus 5.

Yarns A, B and C.
Cast on with A and purl one row.
Row 1 (RS) With B, k2, *sl 1 wyib, k5; rep from *, end sl 1, k2.
Row 2 With B, p4, *sl 3 wyib, p3; rep from *, end p1.
Row 3 With C, k1, *sl 1 wyib, k1, sl 1 wyib, k3; rep from *, end (sl 1, k1) twice.
Row 4 With C, Purl.
Row 5 With A, k1, *sl 3 wyib, k1, insert needle under the loose B strand on front of fabric and knit next st, catching strand behind st, k1; rep from *, end sl 3, k1.
Row 6 With A, p2, *sl 1 wyif, p5; rep from *, end sl 1, p2.
Row 7 With B, k5, *sl 1 wyib, k5; rep from *.
Row 8 With B, p1, *sl 3 wyib, p3; rep from *, end sl 3, pl.
Row 9 With C, k4, *sl 1 wyib, k1, sl 1 wyib, k3; rep from *, end k1.
Row 10 With C, purl.
Row 11 With A, k2, *knit next st under loose B strand (as in row 5), k1, sl 3 wyib, k1; rep from *, end knit next st under loose strand, k2.
Row 12 With A, p5, *sl 1 wyif, p5; rep from *.
Repeat rows 1 to 12.

Thorn

Materials Double knitting yarn for warmth; medium-weight yarn for a deep-textured but firm finish.

Uses All-over pattern for suits, coats and jackets; or snug-fitting hat with matching scarf and gloves.

Multiple of 4 sts plus 1.

Yarns A and B.

Row 1 (RS) With A, k2, ★(k1, yo, k1) in next st, k3; rep from ★, end last repeat k2.

Row 2 With B, p2, ★sl 3 wyif, p3; rep from ★, end last repeat p2.

Row 3 With B, k1, ★k2tog, sl 1 wyib, sl 1, k1, psso, k1; rep from ★.

Row 4 With A, p4, ★sl 1 wyif, p3; rep from ★, end p1.

Row 5 With A, k4, ★(k1, yo, k1) in next st, k3; rep from ★, end k1.

Row 6 With B, p4, ★sl 3 wyif, p3; rep from ★, end p1.

Row 7 With B, k3, ★k2tog, sl 1 wyib, sl 1, k1, psso, k1; rep from ★, end k2.

Row 8 With A, p2, ★sl 1 wyif, p3; rep from ★, end last repeat p2.

Repeat rows 1 to 8.

Embossed rosebud

Materials Medium-weight crepe, novelty mix or acrylic yarn for a summery look; double knitting or mohair for warmth.
Uses Inset panel for dress yoke, teenager's cardigan or pullover; all-over pattern for slipover or waistcoat.

Multiple of 8 sts.

Row 1 (WS) *K3, p2, k3; rep from *.
Row 2 *P3, sl next st to cn and hold at front, k1, yrn 5 times, then k1 from cn, p3; rep from *.
Row 3 *K3, p1, k5tbl, p1, k3; rep from *.
Row 4 *P3, (k1, yfwd) 6 times, k1, p3; rep from *.
Row 5 *K3, p13, k3; rep from *.
Row 6 *P3, k13, p3; rep from *.
Row 7 *K3, p2tog, p9, p2tog tbl, k3; rep from *.

Row 8 *P3, sl 1, k1, psso, k7, k2tog, p3; rep from *.
Row 9 *K3, p2tog, p5, p2tog tbl, k3; rep from *.
Row 10 *P3, sl 1, k1, psso, k3, k2tog, p3; rep from *.
Row 11 *K3, p2tog, p1, p2tog tbl, k3; rep from *.
Row 12 *P3, sl 1, k1, psso, k1, p3; rep from *.
Repeat rows 1 to 12.

Briar rose

Materials Chunky-weight tweed or mohair for a soft, warm effect; Aran-type yarn for a traditional look.

Uses Inset panel for sweater or gloves, baby blanket when combined with lace patterns, border for cardigan front.

Panel of 17 sts.

Note *Left Twist (LT): with right needle behind left needle, miss one st and knit second st through the back. Insert right needle into backs of both the missed st and the second st, and k2tog-b.*
Right Twist (RT): K2tog, leaving sts on left needle. Insert right needle from the front between the two sts knitted together. Knit the first st again, then slip both sts from needle together.

Row 1 (WS) K5, p1, k1, p2, k2, p1, k5.
Row 2 P5, LT, p1, LT, RT, p5.
Row 3 K6, p2, k2, p1, k6.
Row 4 P4, (k1, yo, k1) in next st, turn and p3, turn and k3 wrapping yarn twice for each knit st; p1, LT, p1, RT, p6.
Row 5 K6, p2, k1, p1, k2, sl next 3 sts dropping extra wraps, sl the same 3 sts back to left needle and p3tog-b, k4.
Row 6 P4, LT, p1, k1-b, RT, LT, p5.
Row 7 K5, p1, k2, p2, k1, p1, k5.
Row 8 P5, LT, RT, p1, RT, p5.
Row 9 K6, p1, k2, p2, k6.
Row 10 P6, LT, p1, RT, p1, (k1, yo, k1) in next st, turn and p3, turn and k3 wrapping yarn twice for each knit st, p4.
Row 11 K4, sl next 3 sts dropping extra wraps, sl the same 3 sts back to left needle and p3tog; k2, p1, k1, p2, k6.
Row 12 P5, RT, LT, k1-b, p1, RT, p4.
Repeat rows 1 to 12.

Rosebud

Materials Lightweight wool for a simple effect; angora, mohair-type or silk and linen mix for luxury.

Uses All-over pattern for girl's party dress, baby's bonnet and sweater set or shawl.

Multiple of 16 sts plus 9.

Row 1 *(WS) and all other WS rows* Purl.
Row 2 K10, *k2tog, yo, k1, yo, sl 1, k1, psso, k11; rep from *, end last repeat k10.
Row 4 K9, *k2tog, yo, k3, yo, sl 1, k1, psso, k9; rep from *.
Row 6 K10, *yo, sl 1, k1, psso, yo, k3tog, yo, k11; rep from *, end last repeat k10.
Row 8 K11, *yo, sl 1, k2tog, psso, yo, k13, rep from *, end last repeat k11.
Row 10 K2, *k2tog, yo, k1, yo, sl 1,

k1, psso, k11; rep from *, end last repeat k2.
Row 12 K1, *k2tog, yo, k3, yo, sl 1, k1, psso, k9; rep from *, end last repeat k1.
Row 14 K2, *yo, sl 1, k1, psso, yo, k3tog, yo, k11; rep from *, end last repeat k2.
Row 16 K3, *yo, sl 1, k2tog, psso, yo, k13; rep from *, end last repeat k3.
Repeat rows 1 to 16.

Lily of the valley

Materials Lightweight wool or cotton yarn for baby clothes; lurex or silk and acrylic mix for special occasions.

Uses Christening gown or bridal gown train, all-over pattern for evening jacket or overblouse.

Panel of 27 sts.

To get the Lily of the Valley effect this pattern has to be used in a garment made from the top down. However it is just as pretty when used the other way up.

Note *Make Bobble (MB): (k1, p1, k1, p1, k1) into the same st, making 5 sts from one; then pass the 4th, 3rd, 2nd and first of the new sts separately over the last st made.*

Row 1 *(WS) and all other WS rows* K2, p23, k2.

Row 2 P2, sl 1, k1, psso, k6, (yo, k1) twice, sl 1, k2tog, psso, (k1, yo) twice, k6, k2tog, p2.

Row 4 P2, sl 1, k1, psso, k5, yo, k1, yo, k2, sl 1, k2tog, psso, k2, yo, k1, yo, k5, k2tog, p2.

Row 6 P2, sl 1, k1, psso, k4, yo, k1, yo, MB, k2, sl 1, k2tog, psso, k2, MB, yo, k1, yo, k4, k2tog, p2.

Row 8 P2, sl 1, k1, psso, k3, yo, k1, yo, MB, k3, sl 1, k2tog, psso, k3, MB, yo, k1, yo, k3, k2tog, p2.

Row 10 P2, sl 1, k1, psso, k2, yo, k1, yo, MB, k4, sl 1, k2tog, psso, k4, MB, yo, k1, yo, k2, k2tog, p2.

Row 12 P2, sl 1, k1, psso, (k1, yo) twice, MB, k5, sl 1, k2tog, psso, k5, MB, (yo, k1) twice, k2tog, p2.

Row 14 P2, sl 1, k1, psso, yo, k1, yo, MB, k6, sl 1, k2tog, psso, k6, MB, yo, k1, yo, k2tog, p2.

Repeat rows 1 to 14.

Lotus pattern

Materials Fine crochet cotton for furnishings; lightweight yarn for edgings and borders.

Uses Lacy edge for tablecloths or guest towels; borders for blouse sleeves or collar.

Multiple of 10 sts plus 1.

Note *Sl 2-k1-p2sso: insert needle into fronts of 2nd and first sts on left needle, and slip both. Knit next st on left needle, then insert left needle point into both slipped sts at once and draw them together over the knit stitch and off right needle. Sl2-pl-p2sso: insert needle from left into back loops of 2nd and first sts, and slip both. Purl next st on left needle, then insert left needle point into both slipped sts at once and draw them together over the purled st and off right needle.*

Rows 1, 2, 3, 4 and 5 Knit.

Row 6 (WS) P1, *yo, p3, sl2-pl-p2sso, p3, yo, pl; rep from *.

Row 7 K2, *yo, k2, sl2-k1-p2sso, k2, yo, k3; rep from *, end last repeat k2.

Row 8 P3, *yo, p1, sl2-pl-p2sso, p1, yo, p5; rep from from *, end last repeat p3.

Row 9 K4, *yo, sl2-k1-p2sso, yo, k7; rep from *, end last repeat k4.

Row 10 P2, *k2, p3; rep from *, end last repeat p2.

Row 11 K1, *yo, sl 1, k1, psso, p1, yo, sl2-k1-p2sso, yo, p1, k2tog, yo, k1; rep from *.

Row 12 P3, *k1, p3, k1, p5; rep from *, end last repeat p3.

Row 13 K2, *yo, sl 1, k1, psso, yo, sl 2-k1-p2sso, yo, k2tog, yo, k3; rep from *, end last repeat k2.

Row 14 P2, *k1, p5, k1, p3; rep from *, end last repeat p2.

Row 15 K2, *p1, k1, yo, sl2-kl-p2sso, yo, k1, p1, k3; rep from *, end last repeat k2.

Row 16 As row 14.

Repeat rows 1 to 16.

Harebell

Materials Medium-weight yarn of a single shade, or variegated or flecked mixtures.

Uses All-over pattern for decorative cushion cover or tablecloth; child's skirt or dress with matching scarf.

Multiple of 6 sts plus 3.

Rows 1, 3, and 5 (WS) P3, *k3, p3; rep from *.

Row 2 K3, *p2tog, yrn, p1, k3; rep from *.

Row 4 K3, *p1, yrn, p2tog, k3; rep from *.

Row 6 K1, k2tog, *(p1, yrn) twice, p1, sl 1, k2tog, psso; rep from *, end last repeat sl 1, k1, psso, k1.

Rows 7, 9, and 11 K3, *p3, k3; rep from *.

Row 8 P1, yrn, p2tog, *k3, p1, yrn, p2tog; rep from *.

Row 10 P2tog, yrn, p1, *k3, p2tog, yrn, p1; rep from *.

Row 12 P2, yrn, p1, *sl 1, k2tog, psso, (p1, yrn) twice, p1; rep from * to last 6 sts, sl 1, k2tog, psso, p1, yrn, p2.
Repeat rows 1 to 12.

Three flowers

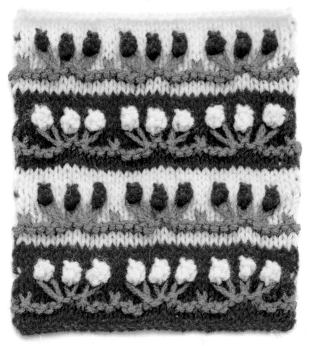

Materials Medium-weight or double knitting yarn; remnants of several shades, if available.

Uses Inset bands for dress yoke, handbag, dirndl or Tyrolean waistcoat; all-over pattern for cushions or blankets.

Multiple of 10 sts plus 3.

Yarns A, B and C.

Note *Make Bobble (MB): p3, turn and k3, turn and sl 1, k2tog, psso.*

Row 1 (RS) With A, knit.

Row 2 With A, purl.

Row 3 With B, knit.

Row 4 With B, k5, *k3 wrapping yarn 3 times for each st, k7; rep from *, end last repeat k5.

Row 5 With A, k1, *sl 1 wyib, k3, sl3 wyib dropping extra wraps, k3; rep from *, end sl 1, k1.

Row 6 With A, p1, *sl 1 wyif, p3, sl 3 wyif, p3; rep from *, end sl 1, p1.

Row 7 With A, k5, *sl 3 wyib, k7; rep from *, end last repeat k5.

Row 8 With A, p5, *sl 3 wyif, p7; rep from *, end last repeat p5.

Row 9 With A, k3, *sl 2 wyib, drop next (1st yarn B) st off needle to front

of work, sl the same 2 sts back to left needle, pick up dropped st and knit it, k3, drop next (3rd yarn B) off needle to front of work, k2, pick up dropped st and knit it, k3; rep from *.

Row 10 With C, p1, sl 2 wyif, *[(p1, k1, p1,) in next st, sl 2 wyif] twice, (p1, k1, p1) in next st, sl 3 wyif; rep from *, end [(p1, k1, p1) in next st. sl 2 wyif] 3 times, p1.

Row 11 With C, k1, sl 2 wyib, *MB in next 3 (increased) sts, (sl 2 wyib, MB) twice, sl 3 wyib; rep from *, end (MB, sl 2 wyib) 3 times, k1.

Row 12 With A, purl, purling into the back of each bobble st.

Rows 13 and 14 With A, repeat rows 1 and 2.

Repeat rows 1 to 14.

Florette bobble

Materials Medium-weight or double knitting yarn in single shade for textured adult pattern; contrasting colours for girl's garments.
Uses All-over pattern for sleeveless pullover or child's party coat; inset panel for pockets or yoke of child's dress.

Multiple of 8 sts.

Note *Make Bobble (MB): (k1, yfwd, k1) in next st, turn, p3, turn, k3, turn, p2tog, p1, turn, sl 1, k1, psso.*
Row 1 (RS) *P3, k1, p4; rep from *.
Row 2 *K4, p1, k3; rep from *.
Row 3 As row 1.
Row 4 As row 2.
Row 5 *P2, MB, k1, MB, p3; rep from *.
Row 6 As row 2.
Row 7 *P3, MB, p4; rep from *.
Row 8 Knit.
Row 9 P7, *k1, p7; rep from * to last st, p1.
Row 10 K8, *p1, k7; rep from *.
Row 11 As row 9.
Row 12 As row 10.
Row 13 P6, *MB, k1, MB, p5; rep from * to last 2 sts, p2.
Row 14 As row 10.
Row 15 P7, *MB, p7; rep from * to last st, p1.
Row 16 Knit.
Repeat rows 1 to 16.

BIRDS BEASTS & BEES

*The airy wings of insects and birds inspired
handknitters to capture their filmy texture
– often in lacy stitches which echoed contemporary
lace fabrics. Even aspects of more earthy animals
could be expressed in quite delicate patterns.*

Flying wings

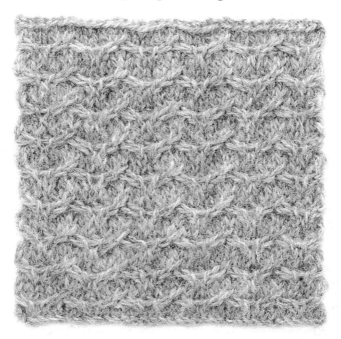

Materials Lightly twisted double knitting yarn for warm, densely textured Arans; chunky yarn for furnishings.
Uses Inset panel for sweater; or combine with other Aran patterns for classic fisherman's jersey or girl's poncho and hat, cushion set panel.

Multiple of 6 sts.

Row 1 (RS) Knit.
Row 2 Purl.
Row 3 *Miss 2 sts, knit into 3rd st on left needle and pull through a loop; then knit first and 2nd sts and sl all 3 sts from needle together; sl next st to dpn and hold in front, k2, then k1 from dpn; rep from *.
Row 4 P5, *miss one st and purl the 2nd st on left needle, then purl the missed st and sl both sts from needle together, p4; rep from *, end p1.
Repeat rows 1 to 4.

Little birds

Materials Medium-weight Shetland or novelty mix for town and country wear; angora, crepe or chenille for luxury.

Uses Inset panel for smock or sweater yoke, or sleeve band; all-over pattern for classic sweater or shawl.

Multiple of 14 sts plus 8.

Row 1 (WS) Purl.
Row 2 Knit.
Row 3 Purl.
Row 4 K10, *sl 2 wyib, k12; rep from *, end last repeat k10.
Row 5 P10, *sl 2 wyif, p12; rep from *, end last repeat p10.
Row 6 K8, *sl 2 wyib, drop first sl st to front of work, sl same 2 sts back to left needle, pick up dropped st and knit it, k2, drop next sl st to front of work, k2, pick up dropped st and knit it, k8; rep from *.
Rows 7, 8 and 9 As rows 1, 2 and 3.
Row 10 K3, *sl 2 wyib, k12; rep from *, end last repeat k3.
Row 11 P3, *sl 2 wyif, p12; rep from *, end last repeat p3.
Row 12 K1, *rep from * of row 6; end last repeat k1.
Repeat rows 1 to 12.

Ostrich plumes

Materials Fine wool or rayon for a classic look; cotton or synthetic yarn for strength and washability.

Uses Inset panel for sweater yoke or pinafore; all-over pattern for curtains, bed or pillow cover.

Multiple of 16 sts plus 1.

Row 1 *(WS) and all other WS rows*
Purl.
Rows 2, 6, 10, 14, 18, 22, 26 and 30
Knit.
Rows 4, 8, 12 and 16 (K1, yo) 3 times, *(sl 1, k1, psso) twice, sl 2 k-wise, k1, p2sso, (k2tog) twice, (yo, k1) 5 times, yo; rep from *, end (sl 1, k1, psso) twice, sl 2 k-wise, k1, p2sso, (k2tog) twice, (yo, k1) 3 times.
Rows 20, 24, 28 and 32 (K2tog) 3 times, *(yo, k1) 5 times, yo, (sl 1, k1, psso) twice, sl 2 k-wise, k1, p2sso, (k2tog) twice; rep from *, end (yo, k1) 5 times, yo, (sl 1, k1, psso) 3 times.
Repeat rows 1 to 32.

Peacocks' tails

Materials Fine or medium-weight Shetland wool, for daywear, silk or rayon for a special party look.

Uses Inset panel for mother and daughter skirts, or all-over pattern for matching party top, jacket or evening scarf.

Panel of 28 sts.

Rows 1 and 3 (RS) knit.
Rows 2 and 4 Purl.
Row 5 K12, k2tog, (yo) twice, sl 1, k1, psso, k12.
Row 6 *and all subsequent WS rows* Purl, working (p1, k1) into every double yo of the preceding row.
Rows, 7, 11, 15, 19, 23 and 27 Knit.
Row 9 K10, (k2tog, yo twice, sl 1, k1, psso) twice, k10.
Row 13 K8, (k2tog, yo twice, sl 1, k1,

psso) 3 times, k8.
Row 17 K6, (k2tog, yo twice, sl 1, k1, psso) 4 times, k6.
Row 21 K4, (k2tog, yo twice, sl 1, k1, psso) 5 times, k4.
Row 25 K2, (k2tog, yo twice, sl 1, k1, psso) 6 times, k2.
Row 29 As row 13.
Row 30 Purl, working (p1, k1) into each double yo.
Repeat rows 1 to 30.

Wings of the swan

Materials Fine angora, light-weight wool, silk or cotton for fine summer days.

Uses Inset panel for kneesocks or legwarmers; all-over pattern for party dress, bridal train or baby's shawl.

Panel of 23 sts.

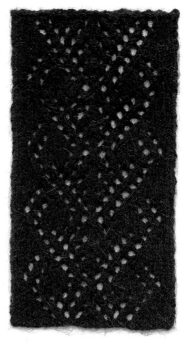

Row 1 (*WS*) *and all other WS rows* Purl.

Row 2 K4, (k2tog, yo) twice, k1, yo, sl 1, k1, psso, k1, k2tog, yo, k1, (yo, sl 1, k1, psso) twice, k4.

Row 4 K3, (k2tog, yo) twice, k1, yo, sl 1, k1, psso, yo, sl 1, k2tog, psso, yo, k2tog, yo, k1, (yo, sl 1, k1, psso) twice, k3.

Row 6 K2, *(k2tog, yo) twice, k1, (yo, sl 1, k1, psso) twice, k1; rep from * once, end k1.

Row 8 K1, (k2tog, yo) twice, k3, yo, sl 1, k1, psso, yo, sl 1, k2tog, psso, yo, k2tog, yo, k3, (yo, sl 1, k1, psso) twice, k1.

Row 10 *K1, (yo, sl 1, k1, psso) twice, k2, (k2tog, yo) twice; rep from * once, end k1.

Row 12 K2, *(yo, sl 1, k1, psso) twice, (k2tog, yo) twice, k3; rep from * once, ending k2 instead of k3.

Row 14 K3, yo, sl 1, k1, psso, (k2tog, yo) twice, k1, yo, sl 1, k2tog, psso, yo, k1, (yo, sl 1, k1, psso) twice, k2tog, yo, k3.

Repeat rows 1 to 14.

Butterfly stitch

Materials Medium-weight yarn, crepe or double knitting wool for a deep-textured fabric with a young look.

Uses All-over pattern for mother and daughter sweaters, toddler's top or baby's blanket; inset panel for coat yoke.

Multiple of 10 sts plus 9.

Rows 1, 3, 5, 7 and 9 (RS) K2, *sl 5 wyif, k5; rep from *, end sl 5, k2.
Rows 2, 4, 6 and 8 Purl.
Row 10 P4, *on the next st (which is at the middle of the slipped group) insert right needle down through the 5 loose strands, bring needle up and transfer the 5 strands to left needle, purl the 5 strands and the next st together as one st, p9; rep from *, end last repeat p4.
Rows 11, 13, 15, 17 and 19 K7, *sl 5 wyif, k5; rep from *, end sl 5, k7.
Rows 12, 14, 16 and 18 Purl.
Row 20 P9, *insert needle down through 5 loose strands, bring them up and purl them together with next st as before, p9; rep from *.
Repeat rows 1 to 20.

Cobweb

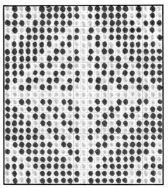

Odd rows are knit rows, even rows are purl rows; the lighter squares are purled on the knit rows and knitted on the purl rows.
Repeat: 23 stitches × 23 rows

Materials Aran-type yarn for a traditional look; medium-weight wool, novelty mix or acrylic for town wear.
Uses Border panels for traditional fishermen's jerseys; all-over patterns for babies' sleeping bags, cardigans or waistcoats.

Butterflies

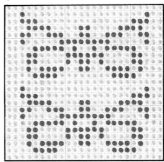

Odd rows are knit rows, even rows are purl rows; the darker squares are purled on the knit rows and knitted on the purl rows.
Repeat: 21 stitches × 11 rows

Materials as above
Uses As above

Honey bee

Materials Fine or medium-weight wool, cotton or acrylic yarn.
Uses Inset panel for stockings or leg-warmers, gloves or evening skirt;
all-over pattern for short-sleeved sweater.

Multiple of 18 sts plus 6.

Note *A and B form panels of faggoting
between the honeybee motifs.*
A : p1, k2, yo, sl 1, k1, psso, p1.
B : k1, p2, yo, p2tog, k1.
Row 1 (RS) *A*, ★k4, k2tog, yo, sl 1,
k1, psso, k4, *A*; rep from ★.
Row 2 *B*, ★p3, p2tog-b, drop the yo of
previous row off the needle, (yo)
twice, p2tog, p3, *B*; rep from ★.
Row 3 *A*, ★k2, k2tog, drop the yos of
previous row off the needle, (yo) 3
times, sl 1, k1, psso, k2, *A*; rep from★.
Row 4 *B*, ★p1, p2tog-b, drop the yos

of previous row off the needle, (yo) 4
times, p2tog, p1, *B*; rep from ★.
Row 5 *A*, ★k2tog, drop the yos of
previous row off the needle, cast on 4
sts on right needle, k1 under the 4
loose strands of the dropped yos; then
yo and k1 again under the 4 loose
strands, cast on 4 sts on right needle,
sl 1, k1, psso, *A*; rep from ★.
Row 6 *B*, ★p5, p2tog (st and following
yo), p6, *B*; rep from ★.
Repeat rows 1 to 6.

Wasp wings

Materials Fine-weight wool, angora or lurex for classic styles; cotton or synthetic for wash and wear.

Uses All-over pattern for christening gown, bridal train or cape; inset panel for evening wrap.

Panel of 13 sts.

Row 1 (RS) P3, k2tog, yo, k1, p1, k1, yo, sl 1, k1, psso, p3.

Row 2 K3, p3, k1, p3, k3.

Row 3 P2, (k2tog, yo) twice, p1, (yo, sl 1, k1, psso) twice, p2.

Row 4 K2, p3, k1-b, k1, k1-b, p3, k2.

Row 5 P1, (k2tog, yo) twice, p3, (yo, sl 1, k1, psso) twice, p1.

Row 6 K1, p3, k1-b, k3, k1-b, p3, k1.

Row 7 P1, yo, sl 1, k2tog, psso, yo, p5, yo, sl 1, k1, psso, slip the sl 1-k1-psso st back to left needle and pass next st over it, then return it to right needle; yo, p1.

Row 8 K1, (k1-b, p1) twice, k3, (p1, k1-b) twice, k1.

Repeat rows 1 to 8.

Cocoon stitch

Materials Thick, medium-weight wool or novelty mix for outdoor wear; angora or mohair for lightweight warmth.

Uses All-over pattern for slip-over or V-neck button-through cardigan, teenager's sweater or baby's sleeping bag.

Multiple of 8 sts plus 1.

Row 1 (WS) P1, *k1, p1, k5, p1; rep from *.
Row 2 K1, *p5, k1, p1, k1; rep from *.
Row 3 P1, *m1, (k1, p1, k1) in next st, m1, p1, p5tog, p1; rep from *.
Rows 4, 6 and 8 K1, *p1, k1, p5, k1; rep from *.
Rows 5 and 7 P1, *k5, p1, k1, p1; rep from *.
Row 9 P1, *p5tog, p1, m1, (k1, p1, k1) in next st, m1, p1; rep from *.
Row 10 As row 2.
Row 11 As row 1.
Row 12 As row 2.
Repeat rows 1 to 12.

Lambs' tails

Materials Hairy, nubby or tweedy yarn for a shaggy effect; double knitting for warmth and texture.
Uses Edging for collar or sleeve; border for sweater, jacket or coat; all-over pattern for ski-caps and mittens.

Multiple of 4 sts plus 1.

Note *Increase 4, decrease 4 (INC 4, DEC 4): knit the st, place new loop on left needle beside the original st; then knit the new loop and place the next new loop on the left needle; repeat until there are 4 new loops on the left needle beside the original st. Then cast off 4 in the usual way, i.e. k2, pass first st over 2nd, knit next st, pass 2nd st over it, and so on until 4 sts have been cast off, the last one being passed over the original st, which is now* on the right needle.
Rows 1 and 2 Knit.
Row 3 (RS) *K3, (INC 4, DEC 4) in next st; rep from *, end k1.
Row 4 K1, *p1, k3; rep from *.
Rows 5 and 6 Knit.
Row 7 K1, *(INC 4, DEC 4) in next st, k3; rep from *.
Row 8 *K3, p1; rep from *, end k1.
Repeat rows 1 to 8.

Bear track

Materials Mohair, angora, alpaca or cashmere-mix yarns for a soft, warm look.

Uses All-over pattern for stole; cape; soft lacy blouse and baby's blanket.

Multiple of 16 sts plus 1.

Row 1 (RS) K1, *yo, (k1, p1) 7 times, k1, yo, k1; rep from *.

Row 2 K1, *p2, (k1, p1) 7 times, p1, k1; rep from *.

Row 3 K2, *yo, (k1, p1) 7 times, k1, yo, k3; rep from *, end last repeat k2.

Row 4 K2, *p2, (k1, p1) 7 times, p1, k3; rep from *, end last repeat k2.

Row 5 K3, *yo, (k1, p1) 7 times, k1, yo, k5; rep from *, end last repeat k3.

Row 6 K3, *p2, (k1, p1) 7 times, p1, k5; rep from *, end last repeat k3.

Row 7 K4, *yo, (k1, p1) 7 times, k1, yo, k7; rep from *, end last repeat k4.

Row 8 K4, *p2, (k1, p1) 7 times, p1, k7; rep from *, end last repeat k4.

Row 9 K5, *(sl 1, k1, psso) 3 times, sl 1, k2tog, psso, (k2tog) 3 times, k9; rep from *, end last repeat k5.

Row 10 Purl.

Repeat rows 1 to 10.

Horseshoe

Materials Medium-weight Shetland yarn for durability; mohair or angora yarn for softness and warmth.

Uses All-over pattern for evening blouse and jacket; edging for sleeves, evening skirt.

Multiple of 10 sts plus 1.

Rows 1 and 3 (WS) Purl.
Row 2 K1, *yo, k3, sl 1, k2tog, psso, k3, yo, k1; rep from *.
Row 4 P1, *k1, yo, k2, sl 1, k2tog, psso, k2, yo, k1, p1; rep from *.
Rows 5 and 7 K1, *p9, k1; rep from*.

Row 6 P1, *k2, yo, k1, sl 1, k2tog, psso, k1, yo, k2, p1; rep from *.
Row 8 P1, *k3, yo, sl 1, k2tog, psso, yo, k3, p1; rep from *.
Repeat rows 1 to 8.

Track of the turtle

Version 1   Version 2

Materials Fine or medium-weight crepe wool or cotton yarn for a summery look; metallic or rayon yarn for evening elegance.

Uses All-over pattern for evening skirt or dress; inset panel for socks and mittens.

Version 1

Panel of 15 sts.

Row 1 *(WS) and all other WS rows* K3, p9, k3.
Row 2 P3, yo, k4, sl 1, k1, psso, k3, p3.
Row 4 P3, k1, yo, k4, sl 1, k1, psso, k2, p3.
Row 6 P3, k2, yo, k4, sl 1, k1, psso, k1, p3.
Row 8 P3, k3, yo, k4, sl 1, k1, psso, p3.
Row 10 P3, k3, k2tog, k4, yo, p3.
Row 12 P3, k2, k2tog, k4, yo, k1, p3.
Row 14 P3, k1, k2tog, k4, yo, k2, p3.
Row 16 P3, k2tog, k4, yo, k3, p3.
Repeat rows 1 to 16.

Version 2

Panel of 15 sts.

Row 1 (WS) K3, p9, k3.
Row 2 P3, yo, k4, sl 1, k1, psso, k3, p3.
Row 3 K3, p2, p2tog-b, p4, yo, p1, k3.
Row 4 P3, k2, yo, k4, sl 1 k1, psso, k1, p3.
Row 5 K3, p2tog-b, p4, yo, p3, k3.
Row 6 P3, k9, p3.
Row 7 K3, yo, p4, p2tog, p3, k3.
Row 8 P3, k2, k2tog, k4, yo, k1, p3.
Row 9 K3, p2, yo, p4, p2tog, p1, k3.
Row 10 P3, k2tog, k4, yo, k3, p3.
Repeat rows 1 to 10.

TREES

All cultures prize trees; not only because they provide food and shelter, but because they often have spiritual significance. The intrinsic properties of a tree – its long and straight growth, its ability to support and regenerate life, and its beauty – are just those that knitters feel worthy to display on their garments.

Welted leaf

Materials Double knitting or Aran-type yarn for a traditional look; novelty mix or crepe for interest.

Uses All-over pattern for blanket, cushion or shoulder bag; border panel for fisherman's jersey, evening skirt or waistcoat.

Multiple of 8 sts.

Row 1 (RS) Knit.
Row 2 Purl.
Row 3 *K4, p4; rep from *.
Row 4 K3, *p4, k4; rep from *, end p4, k1.
Row 5 P2, *k4, p4; rep from *, end k4, p2.
Row 6 K1, *p4, k4; rep from *, end p4, k3.
Row 7 K3, *p4, k4; rep from *, end p4, k1.
Row 8 P2, *k4, p4; rep from *, end k4, p2.
Row 9 K1, *p4, k4; rep from *, end p4, k3.
Row 10 *P4, k4; rep from *.
Row 11 Knit.
Row 12 Purl.
Row 13 Purl.
Row 14 Knit.
Repeat rows 1 to 14.

Acorn

Materials Double knitting or chunky Aran-type yarn for a warm, densely-textured fabric.

Uses All-over pattern for cushion covers; inset panel for woman's pullover or cardigan; combine with other Aran patterns for a classic fisherman's jersey.

Multiple of 10 sts plus 2.

Note *Back Cross (BC) : sl 2 sts to dpn and hold at back, k2, then p2 from dpn. Front Cross (FC) : sl 2 sts to dpn and hold at front, p2, then k2 from dpn.*

Row 1 (RS) K1, p3, k4, *p6, k4; rep from *, end p3, k1.

Row 2 K4, p4, *k6, p4; rep from *, end k4.

Row 3 K1, p1, *BC, insert needle under running thread between st just worked and the next st and (k1, p1) into this thread, FC, p2; rep from * to last 2 sts, end last repeat p1, k1.

Rows 4 and 6 K2, *p2, k2; rep from *.

Row 5 K1, p1, *k2, p2; rep from *, end k2, p1, k1.

Row 7 K2, *sl 1, k1, psso, p6, k2tog, k2; rep from *.

Row 8 K1, p2, k6, *p4, k6; rep from *, end p2, k1.

Row 9 K1, insert needle under running thread and knit once into this thread, *FC, p2, BC, (k1, p1) into running thread; rep from *, end FC, p2, BC, knit once into running thread, k1.

Rows 10 and 12 K1, p1, *k2, p2; rep from *, end k2, p1, k1.

Row 11 K2, *p2, k2; rep from *.

Row 13 K1, p3, *k2tog, k2, sl 1, k1, psso, p6; rep from *, end k2tog, k2, sl 1, k1, psso, p3, k1.

Repeat rows 2 to 13.

Little trees

Materials Medium-weight tweedy or multi-coloured wool for a sporty look; medium-weight cotton for summer tops.
Uses Simple but effective border pattern for child's angel top or dress, or adult's lightweight pullover.

Multiple of 12 sts plus 1.

Row 1 (RS) K1, *p1, k1; rep from *.
Row 2 *and all other WS rows* Knit all knit sts and purl all purl sts.
Rows 3, 5 and 7 P6, *k1, p11; rep from *, end k1, p6.
Row 9 P2, *k1, p3; rep from *, end k1, p2.
Row 11 P2, *k2, p2, k1, p2, k2, p3; rep from *, end last repeat p2.
Row 13 P2, *k3, p3; rep from *, end k3, p2.

Row 15 P2, *k4, p1, k4, p3; rep from *, end last repeat p2.
Row 17 P3, *k7, p5; rep from *, end k7, p3.
Row 19 P4, *k5, p7; rep from *, end k5, p4.
Row 21 P5, *k3, p9; rep from *, end k3, p5.
Row 23 P6, *k1, p11; rep from *, end k1, p6.
Row 25 Purl.

Tree of life 1

Materials Medium-weight Shetland yarn for lightweight pullovers; Aran-type or double knitting yarn for extra warmth.

Uses Inset panel for fisherman's sweater – Aran (top), **Guernsey** (below); motif on child's pullover.

Centre panel of 9 sts.

Note *Back Cross (BC) : sl one st to cn and hold at back, k1tbl, then p1 from cn. Front Cross (FC) : sl one st to cn and hold at front, p1, then k1tbl from cn.*
Row 1 (RS) P3, k3tbl, p3.
Row 2 K3, p3tbl, k3.
Row 3 P2, BC, k1tbl, FC, p2.
Row 4 K2, (p1tbl, k1) twice, p1tbl, k2.
Row 5 P1, BC, p1, k1tbl, p1, FC, p1.
Row 6 K1, p1tbl, (k2, p1tbl) twice, k1.
Row 7 BC, p1, k3tbl, p1, FC.
Row 8 P1tbl, k2, p3tbl, k2, p1tbl.
Row 9 P2, BC, k1tbl, FC, p2.
Repeat rows 4 to 9.

Tree of life 2

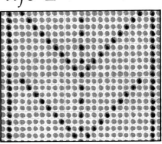

Odd rows are knit rows, even rows are purl rows; the darker squares are purled on the knit rows and knitted on the purl rows.
Repeat: 22 stitches × 10 rows

Materials As above
Uses As above

Banana tree

Materials Medium-weight plain or textured yarn for durability; double knitting or chunky yarn for warmth.

Uses Inset panel for child's or adult's mittens and matching hat set; all-over pattern for cushion cover or blanket.

Panel of 20 sts.

Note *Front Cross (FC) : sl 1 st to cn and hold at front, p1, then k1 from cn.*
Front Knit Cross (FKC) : sl 1 st to cn and hold at front, k1, then k1 from cn.
Front Purl Cross (FPC) : sl 1 st to cn and hold at front, p1, then p1 from cn.
Back Cross (BC) : sl 1 st to cn and hold at back, k1, then p1 from cn.
Back Knit Cross (BKC) : sl 1 st to cn and hold at back, k1, then k1 from cn.
Back Purl Cross (BPC) : sl 1 st to cn and hold at back, p1, then p1 from cn.

Row 1 (WS) K3, p3, k3, p4, BPC, k5.
Row 2 P4, BKC, k1, BC, k2, p3, FC, k1, p3.
Row 3 K3, p2, k4, p2, k1, p3, BPC, k3.
Row 4 P3, k3, BC, p1, k1, FKC, p3, FC, p3.
Row 5 K7, FPC, p2, k2, p4, k3.
Row 6 P3, k2, BC, p2, k1, (FKC) twice, p6.
Row 7 K5, FPC, p4, k3, p3, k3.
Row 8 P3, k1, BC, p3, k2, FC, k1, FKC, p4.
Row 9 K3, FPC, p3, k1, p2, k4, p2, k3.
Row 10 P3, BC, p3, BKC, k1, p1, FC, k3, p3.
Row 11 K3, p4, k2, p2, BPC, k7.
Row 12 P6, (BKC) twice, k1, p2, FC, k2, p3.
Repeat rows 1 to 12.

Hollow oak

Materials Double knitting or Aran-type yarn for a traditional look; medium-weight cashmere for comfort and warmth; novelty mix for a single panel.

Uses Combined with other Aran patterns for traditional fisherman's jersey; inset panel for fancy legwarmers or stockings, decorative braces.

Panel of 17 sts.

Note *Make Bobble (MB): (k1, p1, k1, p1, k1, p1, k1) in one st, making 7 sts from 1, then with point of left needle pass the 2nd, 3rd, 4th, 5th, 6th and 7th sts on right needle separately over the last st made, completing bobble.*
Front Cross (FC): sl 2 sts to cn and hold at front, p1, then k2 from cn.
Back Cross (BC): sl 1 st to cn and hold at back, k2, then p1 from cn.

Rows 1, 3, 5 and 7 (WS) K6, p5, k6.
Row 2 P6, k2, MB, k2, p6.
Row 4 P6, MB, k3, MB, p6.
Row 6 As row 2.
Row 8 P5, BC, p1, FC, p5.
Row 9 K5, p2, k1, p1, k1, p2, k5.
Row 10 P4, BC, k1, p1, k1, FC, p4.
Row 11 K4, p3, k1, p1, k1, p3, k4.
Row 12 P3, BC, (p1, k1) twice, p1, FC, p3.
Row 13 K3, p2, (k1, p1) 3 times, k1, p2, k3.
Row 14 P3, k3, (p1, k1) twice, p1, k3, p3.
Rows 15, 17 and 19 As rows 13, 11 and 9.
Row 16 P3, FC, (p1, k1) twice, p1, BC, p3.
Row 18 P4, FC, k1, p1, k1, BC, p4.
Row 20 P5, FC, p1, BC, p5.
Repeat rows 1 to 20.

Fir trees

Materials Rayon, silk or flecked yarn for a glittering look; medium-weight crochet cotton for durability.

Uses All-over pattern for festive shawl, jacket, cushion cover, tray or tablecloth.

Multiple of 16 sts plus 1.

Row 1 *(WS) and all other WS rows*
Purl.

Row 2 K1, *k5, k2tog, yo, k1, yo, sl 1, k1, psso, k6; rep from *.

Row 4 K1, *k4, k2tog, yo, k3, yo, sl 1, k1, psso, k5; rep from *.

Row 6 K1, *k3 (k2tog, yo) twice, k1, (yo, sl 1, k1, psso) twice, k4; rep from *.

Row 8 K1, *k2, (k2tog, yo) twice, k3, (yo, sl 1, k1, psso) twice, k3; rep from *.

Row 10 K1, *k1, (k2tog, yo) 3 times, k1, (yo, sl 1, k1, psso) 3 times, k2; rep from *.

Rows 12, 14, 16, 18, 20, 22, 24 and 26
As rows 8, 6, 4, 6, 8, 6, 4 and 2.

Row 28 K1, *k6, k2tog, yo, k8; rep from *.

Row 30 K1, *yo, sl 1, k1, psso, k11, k2tog, yo, k1; rep from *.

Row 32 K1, *k1, yo, sl 1, k1, psso, k9, k2tog, yo, k2; rep from *.

Row 34 K1, *(yo, sl 1, k1, psso) twice, k7, (k2tog, yo) twice, k1; rep from *.

Row 36 K1, *k1, (yo, sl 1, k1, psso) twice, k5, (k2tog, yo) twice, k2; rep from *.

Row 38 K1, *(yo, sl 1, k1, psso) 3 times, k3, (k2tog, yo) 3 times, k1; rep from *.

Rows 40, 42, 44, 46, 48, 50, 52 and 54
As rows 36, 34, 32, 34, 36, 34, 32, and 30.

Row 56 K15, *k2tog, yo, k14; rep from * to last 2 sts, end k2.

Repeat rows 1 to 56.

Cherry tree

Materials Lightweight wool, cashmere or silk and linen mix for evening wear; baby yarn for child's garment.

Uses All-over pattern for woman's stole or evening sweater, baby's dress or bonnet and jacket set.

Multiple of 18 sts plus 1.

Note *Front Cross (FC) : sl 1 st to dpn and hold at front, p2, then k1 from dpn. Back Cross (BC) : sl 2 sts to dpn and hold at back, k1, then p2 from dpn.*

Row 1 (WS) K1, *p6, k5, p6, k1; rep from *.

Row 2 P1, *k3, BC, p5, FC, k3, p1; rep from *.

Row 3 K1, *p4, k9, p4, k1; rep from *.

Row 4 P1, *FC, k1, p1, (yo, p2tog) 4 times, k1, BC, p1; rep from *.

Row 5 K3, *p6, k1, p6, k5; rep from *, end last repeat k3.

Row 6 P3, *FC, k3, p1, k3, BC, p5; rep from *, end last repeat p3.

Row 7 K5, *p4, k1, p4, k9; rep from *, end last repeat k5.

Row 8 P1, *(yo, p2tog) twice, k1, BC, p1, FC, k1, p1, (yo, p2tog) twice; rep from *.

Repeat rows 1 to 8.

Willow

Materials Mohair and lightweight yarns for softness; lurex mix for a glittery effect.

Uses All-over pattern for baby's blanket or shawl; inset panel for socks or evening jacket.

Multiple of 10 sts plus 3.

Row 1 K2, *yfwd, k3, sl 1, k2tog, psso, k3, yfwd, k1; rep from *, end k1.

Row 2 *and all other even-numbered rows* Purl.

Row 3 K2, *k1, yfwd, k2, sl 1, k2tog, psso, k2, yfwd, k2; rep from *, end k1.

Row 5 K2, *k2, yfwd, k1, sl 1, k2tog, psso, k1, yfwd, k3; rep from *, end k1.

Row 7 K2, *k3, yfwd, sl 1, k2tog, psso, yfwd, k4; rep from *, end k1.

Row 8 Purl.

Repeat rows 1 to 8.

Fir cone

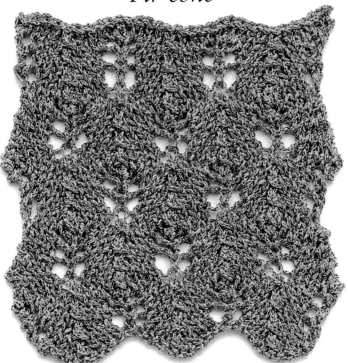

Materials Lightweight crepe wool or cotton yarn for a summery look; metallic or rayon for evening elegance.

Uses All-over pattern for collared sweater, sleeveless overblouse or loose-fitting jacket or shawl.

Multiple of 10 sts plus 1.

Row 1 *(WS) and all other WS rows* Purl.
Rows 2, 4, 6 and 8 K1, *yo, k3, sl 1, k2tog, psso, k3, yo, k1; rep from *.
Rows 10, 12, 14 and 16 K2tog, *k3, yo, k1, yo, k3, sl 1, k2tog, psso; rep from *, end k3, yo, k1, yo, k3, sl 1, k1, psso.
Repeat rows 1 to 16.

Twin leaf lace

Materials Fine angora, lightweight wool, silk or cotton for a luxury look.

Uses Inset panel for smock or pinafore; all-over pattern for child's party dress, woman's twin set or bed jacket.

Panel of 23 sts.

Row 1 (RS) K8, k2tog, yo, k1, p1, k1, yo, sl 1, k1, psso, k8.
Row 2 P7, p2tog-b, p2, yo, k1, yo, p2, p2tog, p7.
Row 3 K6, k2tog, k1, yo, k2, p1, k2, yo, k1, sl 1, k1, psso, k6.
Row 4 P5, p2tog-b, p3, yo, p1, k1, p1, yo, p3, p2tog, p5.
Row 5 K4, k2tog, k2, yo, k3, p1, k3, yo, k2, sl 1, k1, psso, k4.
Row 6 P3, p2tog-b, p4, yo, p2, k1,

p2, yo, p4, p2tog, p3.
Row 7 K2, k2tog, k3, yo, k4, p1, k4, yo, k3, sl 1, k1, psso, k2.
Row 8 P1, p2tog-b, p5, yo, p3, k1, p3, yo, p5, p2tog, p1.
Row 9 K2tog, k4, yo, k5, p1, k5, yo, k4, sl 1, k1, psso.
Row 10 P11, k1, p11.
Row 11 K11, p1, k11.
Row 12 P11, k1, p11.
Repeat rows 1 to 12.

Travelling vine

Materials Medium-weight wool for warmth; silk, synthetic mix or angora for evening wear.

Uses All-over pattern for baby's shawl or blanket, woman's evening sweater or stole; inset panel for knee socks.

Multiple of 8 sts plus 4.

Row 1 (RS) K2, *yo, k1-b, yo, sl 1, k1, psso, k5; rep from *, end k2.
Row 2 P6, *p2tog-b, p7; rep from *, end last repeat p5.
Row 3 K2, *yo, k1-b, yo, k2, sl 1, k1, psso, k3; rep from *, end k2.
Row 4 P4, *p2tog-b, p7; rep from *.
Row 5 K2, *k1-b, yo, k4, sl 1, k1, psso, k1, yo; rep from *, end k2.
Row 6 P3, *p2tog-b, p7; rep from *, end p1.
Row 7 K2, *k5, k2tog, yo, k1-b, yo; rep from *, end k2.
Row 8 P5, *p2tog, p7; rep from *, end last repeat p6.
Row 9 K2, *k3, k2tog, k2, yo, k1-b, yo; rep from *, end k2.
Row 10 *P7, p2tog; rep from *, end p4.
Row 11 K2, *yo, k1, k2tog, k4, yo, k1-b; rep from *, end k2.
Row 12 P1, *p7, p2tog; rep from *, end p3.
Repeat rows 1 to 12.

Ivy leaf

Materials Fine wool, lightweight rayon or cotton yarn for summer sportswear.

Uses All-over pattern for T-shirt, necktie, overblouse or short-sleeved pullover.

Multiple of 10 sts plus 5.

Row 1 Sl 1, k1, *p1, k2, k2tog, yfwd, k1, yfwd, sl 1, k1, psso, k2; rep from * to last 3 sts, p1, k2.

Rows 2, 4 and 6 Sl 1, k1, *k1, p9; rep from * to last 3 sts, k3.

Row 3 Sl 1, k1, *p1, k1, k2tog, k1, yfwd, k1, yfwd, k1, sl 1, k1, psso, k1; rep from * to last 3 sts, p1, k2.

Row 5 Sl 1, k1, *p1, k2tog, k2, yfwd, k1, yfwd, k2, sl 1, k1, psso; rep from * to last 3 sts, p1, k2.

Row 7 Sl 1, k1, *k1, yfwd, sl 1, k1, psso, k2, p1, k2, k2tog, yfwd; rep from * to last 3 sts, k3.

Rows 8, 10 and 12 Sl 1, k1, *p5, k1, p4; rep from * to last 3 sts, p1, k2.

Row 9 Sl 1, k1, *k1, yfwd, k1, sl 1, k1, psso, k1, p1, k1, k2tog, k1, yfwd; rep from * to last 3 sts, k3.

Row 11 Sl 1, k1, *k1, yfwd, k2, sl 1, k1, psso, p1, k2tog, k2, yfwd; rep from * to last 3 sts, k3.

Repeat rows 1 to 12.

Travelling leaf

Materials Lightweight crochet cotton to bring out the pattern; mohair or angora for a fluffy look.

Uses Inset panel for evening blouse or gloves; all-over pattern for poncho, baby's blanket or loose-fitting jacket.

Multiple of 12 sts plus 5.

Row 1 (*WS*) *and all other WS rows*
Purl.
Rows 2 and 4 K2, *k1, yo, k3, k2tog, k1, sl 1, k1, psso, k3, yo; rep from *, end k3.

Rows 6 and 8 K2, *k1, sl 1, k1, psso, k3, yo, k1, yo, k3, k2tog; rep from *, end k3.
Repeat rows 1 to 8.

SEA & SAILORS

*The nature of the water they worked upon, the
life they found in it, and the tools of their
trade were worked by sailors into their traditional
fishermen's sweaters. Wives and sweethearts
included, too, tokens of affection in their men's
jerseys and transferred the often masculine motifs
to their own lacy shawls and blouses.*

Lucina shell

Materials Lightweight cotton or linen for summer wear; baby yarn or
fine-weight wool for cooler evenings.
Uses All-over pattern for shawl, scarf, blouse or fancy sweater; edging
for sock tops.

Multiple of 9 sts plus 3.

Row 1(RS) K2, *yo, k8, yo, k1; rep
from *, end k1.
Row 2 K3, *p8, k3; rep from *.
Row 3 K3, *yo, k8, yo, k3; rep from *.
Row 4 K4, *p8, k5; rep from *, end last
repeat k4.
Row 5 K4, *yo, k8, yo, k5; rep from

*, end last repeat k4.
Row 6 K5, *p8, k7; rep from *, end last
repeat k5.
Row 7 K5, *k4tog-b, k4tog, k7; rep
from *, end last repeat k5.
Row 8 Knit.

Repeat rows 1 to 8.

Seaweed

Materials Light or medium-weight yarn for textural interest; angora or cashmere for warmth and comfort.

Uses The pattern can be used either side but a more undulant shape forms if even-numbered rows are on front side. Effective on blankets and throws or woman's evening skirt or jacket.

Multiple of 6 sts.

Row 1 *P4, k2; rep from *.
Rows 2 *and all other even-numbered rows* Knit all knit sts and purl all purl sts.
Row 3 *P3, k3; rep from *.
Row 5 *P2, k4; rep from *.
Row 7 P1, *k4, p2; rep from *, end k4, p1.
Row 9 P1, *k3, p3; rep from *, end k3, p2.
Row 11 P1, *k2, p4; rep from *, end k2, p3.
Row 12 See row 2.
Repeat rows 1 to 12.

Marriage lines

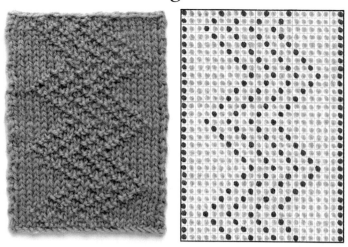

Materials Smooth medium-weight yarn for a classic style.
Uses Panels of this traditional Guernsey pattern can be combined with others on a fisherman's pullover, or used on cushions, window seat covers and children's sweaters.

Odd rows are knit rows, even rows are purl rows; the darker squares are purled on the knit rows and knitted on the purl rows.
Repeat: 21 stitches × 12 rows

Lighthouse

Materials Smooth medium-weight yarn for a classic style.
Uses Panels of this traditional Guernsey pattern can be combined with others on a fisherman's pullover, or used on cushions, window seat covers and children's sweaters.

Odd rows are knit rows, even rows are purl rows; the lighter squares are purled on the knit rows and knitted on the purl rows.
Repeat: 18 stitches × 24 rows

Anchor

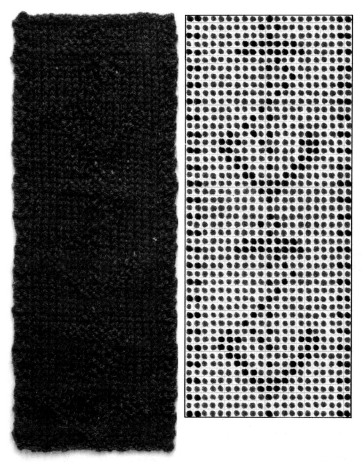

Materials Smooth medium-weight yarn for a classic style.
Uses Panels of this traditional Guernsey pattern can be combined with others on a fisherman's pullover, or used on cushions, window seat covers and children's sweaters.

Odd rows are knit rows, even rows are purl rows; the darker squares are purled on the knit rows and knitted on the purl rows.
Repeat: 18 stitches × 24 rows

Clam shells

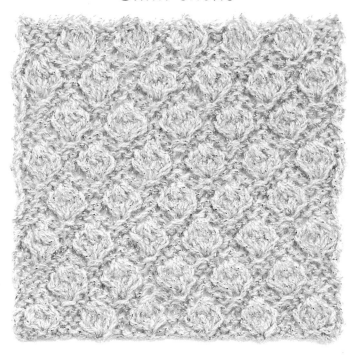

Materials Lurex mix or flecked yarn for a sophisticated look; angora or baby yarn for infant's wear.

Uses All-over pattern for evening jacket, bolero or bag; or baby's bonnet and cardigan set.

Multiple of 4 sts plus 1.

Row 1 (WS) K2, *(p1, yo, p1, yo, p1) in next st, k3; rep from *, end last repeat k2.

Row 2 P2, *k5, p3; rep from *, end last repeat p2.

Row 3 K2, *p5, k3; rep from *, end last repeat k2.

Row 4 P2, *k5tog-b, p3; rep from *, end last repeat p2.

Row 5 K4, *(p1, yo, p1, yo, p1) in next st, k3; rep from *, end k1.

Row 6 P4, *k5, p3; rep from *, end p1.

Row 7 K4, *p5, k3; rep from *, end k1.

Row 8 P4, *k5tog-b, p3; rep from *, end p1.

Repeat rows 1 to 8.

Shell dip stitch

Materials Smooth medium-weight yarn in a single shade, or combined with mohair, angora or lurex mix as a contrast.

Uses All-over pattern in single shade for textured look on pullovers and cardigans; contrasting colours make it effective on evening jacket, skirt or stole.

Multiple of 14 sts plus 2.

Yarns A and B.
Cast on with yarn A and knit one row.
Rows 1, 2, 3, 4, 5 and 6 With B, knit.
Row 7 (RS) With A, k9, *(insert crochet hook into the front of st 5 rows below the 3rd st on left needle, and draw through a long loop, sl this loop on right needle, then knit the next st) 6 times, taking all 6 loops from the same st below, k8; rep from *, end last repeat k1.

Row 8 With A, k1, *(p2tog-b) 3 times, p1, (p2tog) 3 times, k7; rep from *, end k1.
Rows 9, 10, 11, 12, 13 and 14 With B, knit.
Row 15 With A, k2; rep from * of row 7 across.
Row 16 With A, k8, *(p2tog-b) 3 times, p1, (p2tog) 3 times, k7; rep from *, end last repeat k1.
Repeat rows 1 to 16.

Springing cable

Materials Chunky or heavyweight yarn for holiday cruising; angora or mohair for lightweight warmth.

Uses Inset panel for roomy, hooded sweater; child's sleeveless pullover; V-neck cardigan; or snug-fitting hat with matching mittens.

Centre panel of 28 sts.

Note *Front Cross (FC) : sl 3 sts to cn and hold at front, k3, then k3 from cn. Double Front Cross (DFC) : sl 3 sts to cn and hold at front, p2, then k3 from cn. Double Back Cross (DBC) : sl 2 sts to cn and hold at back, k3, then p2 from cn. Triple Front Cross (TFC): sl 3 sts to cn and hold at front, p2, k3, then k3 from cn. Triple Back Cross (TBC): sl 5 sts to cn and hold at back, k3, then k3, p2, from cn.*

Row 1 (RS) K3, DFC, p12, DBC, k3.
Row 2 *and all other even-numbered rows* Knit all the purl sts of the previous row and purl all the knit sts.
Row 3 K3, p2, DFC, p8, DBC, p2, k3.
Row 5 K3, p4, DFC, p4, DBC, p4, k3.
Row 7 K3, p6, DFC, DBC, p6, k3.
Row 9 DFC, p6, FC, p6, DBC.
Row 11 P2, DFC, p4, k6, p4, DBC, p2.
Row 13 P4, DFC, p2, k6, p2, DBC, p4.
Row 15 P6, DFC, FC, DBC, p6.
Row 17 P6, TBC, TFC, p6.
Rows 19 and 21 P6, k6, p4, k6, p6.
Row 23 P4, TBC, p4, TFC, p4.
Rows 25 and 27 P4, k6, p8, k6, p4.
Row 29 P2, TBC, p8, TFC, p2.
Rows 31 and 33 P2, k6, p12, k6, p2.
Row 35 TBC, p12, TFC.
Row 36 P6, k16, p6.
Repeat rows 1 to 36

Open braid cable

Materials Double knitting yarn for thick, warm appearance; medium-weight yarn for everyday wear.

Uses Inset panel for winter-weight man's pullover or with finer yarn as detail on ladies knee socks or leg warmers.

Centre panel of 18 sts.

Note *Back Cross (BC): sl 2 sts to cn and hold at back, k2, then k2 from cn.*
Front Cross (FC): sl 2 sts to cn and hold at front, k2, then k2 from cn.
Single Back Cross (SBC): sl 1 st to cn and hold at back, k2, then p1 from cn.
Single Front Cross (SFC): sl 2 sts to cn and hold at front, p1, then k2 from cn.
Row 1 (WS) K6, p6, k6.
Rows 2, 6 and 10 P6, BC, p6.
Row 3 *and all subsequent odd-numbered rows* Knit the purls sts of the previous row and purl the knit sts.
Rows 4, 8 and 12 P6, FC, k2, p6.
Row 14 P5, SBC, k2, SFC, p5.

Row 16 P4, SBC, p1, k2, p1, SFC, p4.
Row 18 P3, SBC, p2, k2, p2, SFC, p3.
Row 20 P3, SFC, p2, k2, p2, SBC, p3.
Row 22 P4, SFC, p1, k2, p1, SBC, p4.
Row 24 P5, SFC, k2, SBC, p5.
Repeat rows 1 to 24.

Lobster claw cable

Materials Medium to heavy-weight yarn for snug seaside holiday wear; medium-weight cotton for summer wear.

Uses Inset panel for sou'wester and cape or country-style coat; border for tennis pullover.

Panel of 16 sts.

Row 1 (WS) Knit.
Row 2 P4, k1, p6, k1, p4.
Rows 3, 5 and 7 K4, p2, k4, p2, k4.
Rows 4 and 6 P4, k2, p4, k2, p4.
Row 8 P4, slip next 2 sts to cn and hold at front, p2, yfwd, k2tog tbl from cn, slip next 2 sts to cn and hold at back, k2tog, yrn, p2 from cn, p4.
Repeat rows 1 to 8.

Gull stitch

Gull stitch   **Triple gull stitch**   **Inverted gull stitch**

Materials Double knitting or Aran-type yarn for winter wear; medium-weight flecked or tweedy yarn for spring and autumn.

Uses These three patterns can be used in combination as panels for man's pullover or woman's twin set, or singly as all-over patterns for sleeveless pullover or buttoned waistcoat.

Gull stitch

Panel of 10 sts.

Row 1 (WS) K2, p6, k2.
Row 2 P2, k2, sl 2 wyib, k2, p2.
Row 3 K2, p2, sl 2 wyif, p2, k2.
Row 4 P2, sl next 2 sts to cn and hold at back, k1, then k2 from cn, sl next st to cn and hold at front, k2, then k1 from cn, p2.
Repeat rows 1 to 4.

Triple Gull Stitch

Panel of 10 sts.

Rows 1, 3 and 11 (RS) P2, k6, p2.
Row 2 K2, p6, k2.
Row 4 K2, p2, sl 2 wyif, p2, k2.
Row 5 P2, sl next 2 sts to cn and hold at back, k1, k2 from cn, sl next st to cn and hold at front, k2, k1 from cn, p2.
Rows 6, 7, 8 and 9 Repeat rows 4 and 5 twice more.
Rows 10 and 12 K2, p6, k2.
Repeat rows 1 to 12.

Inverted Gull Stitch

Panel of 13 sts.

Rows 1 and 3 (WS) K2, p9, k2.
Row 2 P2, sl next st to cn and hold at front, k3, then k1 from cn, k1, sl next 3 sts to cn and hold at back, k1, then k3 from cn, p2.
Row 4 P2, k9, p2.
Repeat rows 1 to 4.

Valentine cable

Materials Chunky novelty mix or tweedy wool for autumn and winter wear; medium-weight cotton for child's garment.

Uses Single inset panel or repeat with contrast patterns for fisherman's sweater, belted coat or matching hat and scarf; border panel for girl's dress.

Centre panel of 16 sts.

Note *Back Cross (BC) : sl 1 st to cn and hold at back, k2, then p1 from cn.*
Front Cross (FC) : sl 2 sts to cn and hold at front, p1, then k2 from cn.
Single Front Cross (SFC) : sl 1 st to cn and hold at front, p1, then k1 from cn.
Single Back Cross (SBC) : sl 1 st to cn and hold at back, k1, then p1 from cn.

Row 1 and 3 (WS) K6, p4, k6.
Row 2 P6, sl next 2 sts to cn and hold at front, k2, then k2 from cn, p6.
Row 4 P5, BC, FC, p5.
Row 5 K5, p2, k2, p2, k5.
Row 6 P4, BC, p2, FC, p4.
Row 7 (K4, p2) twice, k4.
Row 8 P3, BC, p4, FC, p3.
Row 9 K3, p2, k6, p2, k3.
Row 10 P2, (BC) twice, (FC) twice, p2.
Row 11 K2, (p2, k1, p2, k2) twice.
Row 12 P1, (BC) twice, p2, (FC) twice, p1.
Row 13 (K1, p2) twice, k4, (p2, k1) twice.
Row 14 P1, k1, SFC, FC, p2, BC, SBC, k1, p1.
Row 15 (K1, p1) twice, k1, p2, k2, p2, k1, (p1, k1) twice.
Row 16 P1, k1, p1, SFC, FC, BC, SBC, p1, k1, p1.
Row 17 K1, p1, k2, p1, k1, p4, k1, p1, k2, p1, k1.
Row 18 P1, SFC, SBC, p1, sl next 2 sts to cn and hold at front, k2, then k2 from cn, p1, SFC, SBC, p1.
Row 19 K2, sl next st to cn and hold at back, k1, then k1 from cn, k2, p4, k2, sl next st to cn and hold at front, k1, then k1 from cn, k2.
Repeat rows 4 to 19.

Little wave

Materials Medium-weight yarn; plain, flecked or multi-coloured for close-fitting garments; double knitting for outerwear.
Uses All-over pattern for suit or day dress, ski sweater or sports jacket.

Multiple of 6 sts plus 1.

Note *Right Twist (RT) : k2tog, leaving sts on left needle. Insert right needle from the front between the two sts knitted together. Knit the first st again, then slip both sts from needle together.*
Left Twist (LT) : with right needle behind left needle, miss one st and knit second st through the back. Insert right needle into backs of both the missed st and the second st, and k2tog-b.
Row 1 (RS) Knit.
Row 2 P2, *k2, p4; rep from *, end k2, p3.
Row 3 K2, *LT, k4; rep from *, end LT, k3.

Row 4 P2, *k1, p1, k1, p3; rep from *, end last repeat p2.
Row 5 K3, *LT, k4; rep from *, end LT, K2.
Row 6 P3, *k2, p4; rep from *, end k2, p2.
Row 7 Knit.
Rows 8 and 10 As rows 6 and 4.
Rows 9 K3, *RT, k4; rep from *, end RT, k2.
Row 11 K2, *RT, k4; rep from *, end RT, k3.
Row 12 As row 2.
Repeat rows 1 to 12.

Sea foam

Materials Fine mohair, angora or cashmere wool for garments; fine cotton for furnishings.
Uses All-over pattern for bed jacket, peignoir, overskirt, baby's shawl, tablecloth or placemats.

Multiple of 10 sts plus 6.

Rows 1 and 2 Knit.
Row 3 (RS) K6, *(yo) twice, k1, (yo) 3 times, k1, (yo) 4 times, k1, (yo) 3 times, k1, (yo) twice, k6; rep from *.
Row 4 Knit, dropping all yos off needle.

Rows 5 and 6 Knit.
Row 7 K1; rep from * of row 3, end last repeat k1 instead of k6.
Row 8 As row 4.
Repeat rows 1 to 8.

Old shale

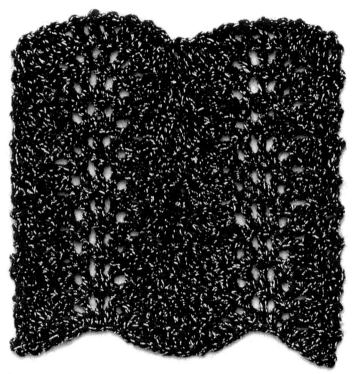

Materials Fine-weight Shetland or cotton yarn to show off pattern; lurex mix for a glittery effect.
Uses All-over pattern for shawl, baby's gown or evening skirt; edging for sleeves, collars and hems.

Multiple of 18 sts.

Row 1 (RS) Knit.
Row 2 Purl.
Row 3 *(K2tog) 3 times, (yo, k1) 6 times, (k2tog) 3 times; rep from *.
Row 4 Knit.
Repeat rows 1 to 4.

HEARTS & SNOWFLAKES

*Intricate colourwork patterns have traditionally
been associated with Scandinavian and Fair-Isle
knitting – not surprisingly since it was the
early sea-faring Norwegians who brought their
traditional patterns to the British Isles. The
snowflakes of the wintry north are often combined with the religiously-inspired hearts.*

Hearts 1

Materials Medium-weight yarn in a variety of shades.
Uses Border panel for skirt or traditional pullover.

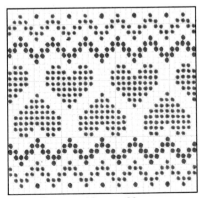

Repeat: 12 sts × 33 rows

Hearts 2

Materials Medium-weight Shetland or synthetic yarn in various shades.

Uses Inset panel for adult's waistcoat or pullover; border for scarf with matching mittens or gloves; single panel for braces.

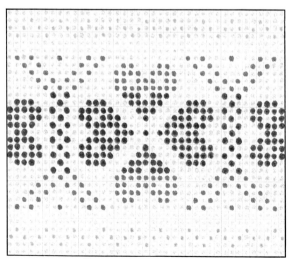

Repeat: 24 sts × 33 rows

Hearts 3

Materials Medium-weight Shetland or synthetic yarn for durability; cotton for child's garments or furnishings.

Uses Border panel for adult's pullover or skirt; single motif for child's pocket or yoke; repeat motif for tablecloth or runner.

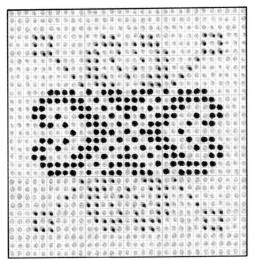

Repeat: 31 sts × 31 rows

Snowflake 1

Materials Fine Shetland yarn for spring wear; medium-to-heavy-weight wool for winter skiing.

Uses All-over repeat for classic pullover; inset bands for chest and sleeves of ski sweater with matching bobble hat, scarf and mittens.

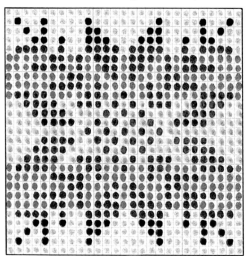

Repeat: 27 sts × 27 rows

Snowflake 2

Materials Shetland wool or medium-weight yarn for weekend wear; heavyweight or chunky yarn for a winter sport look.

Uses Inset band for multi-patterned sweater or jacket, repeat motif for gloves or mittens with matching cap.

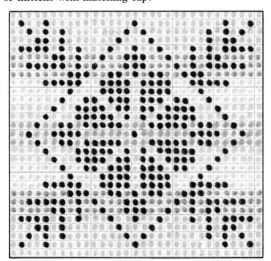

Repeat: 31 sts × 29 rows

Snowflake 3

Materials Fine-weight or baby yarn for infant's garments: medium-weight synthetic or Shetland yarn for furnishings.
Uses Inset band for child's hooded cardigan or sweater yoke; single or repeat motif for cushions or afghans.

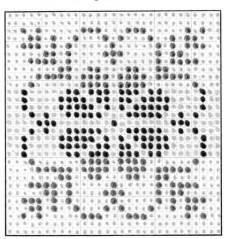

Repeat: 29 sts × 29 rows

FIGURES & MOTIFS

More graphic representations of creatures, objects and experiences from everyday life have always delighted the young and brought great charm to handmade garments. The rendering of certain figures is made even more remarkable when one considers the limitations of the knitting process.

Little men

Materials Medium-weight synthetic or Shetland yarn in various shades.

Uses Border panel for skirt, child's jumper or lederhosen; pencil case or schoolbag cover.

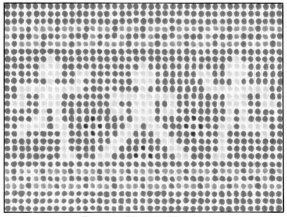

Repeat: 39 sts × 28 rows

Little lady

Materials Angora or mohair wool for a party look; cotton for easy-care summer garments.

Uses Repeat motif as border for child's party dress or skirt; single motif for yoke, pocket or purse.

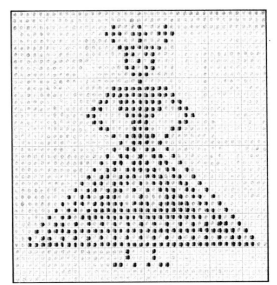

Repeat: 39 sts × 40 rows

Dancing ladies

Materials Double knitting yarn for warmth; medium-weight wool or cotton for child's garments; heavy-weight cotton for furnishing.
Uses Border panel for woman's evening skirt or dressing gown; single motif for yoke of girl's dress; decorative panel for placemats or tablecloth.

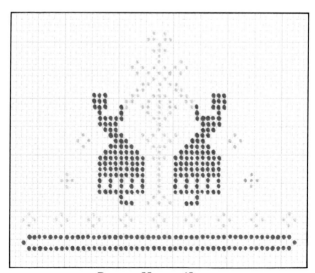

Repeat: 55 sts × 45 rows

Sunburst

Materials Textured cotton or linen and cotton mix for easy-care; medium-weight yarn for warmer garments.

Uses Single motif for pocket, individual coasters, egg cosies, or yoke of child's dress; repeat panel for table runner; border for skirt or jacket.

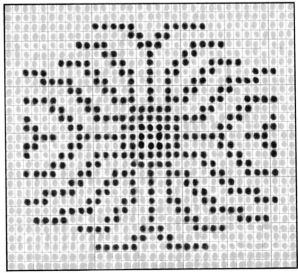

Repeat: 33 sts × 29 rows

Skier

Materials Double knitting or chunky yarn for winter ski gear; medium-weight yarn for small-scale pattern repeats.

Uses Central motif for skier's pullover with matching scarf or child's mittens; repeat motif for hot water bottle cover.

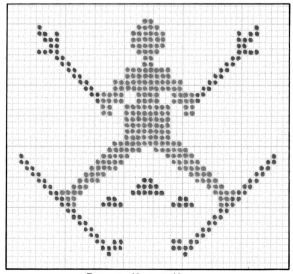

Repeat: 48 sts × 43 rows

Christmas tree

Materials Medium-weight flecked yarn or lurex-mix for a sparkling effect; plain wool or synthetic yarn for day wear.

Uses Repeat motif for festive scarf, skirt border or jacket; or inset panel for Christmas stocking or child's toy bag.

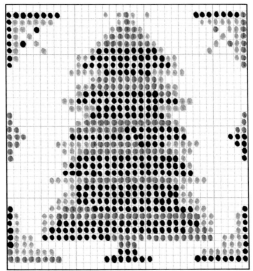

Repeat: 35 sts × 37 rows

Reindeer

Materials Medium-weight yarns of different finishes – mohair, glitter and flecked yarns in addition to simple Shetland wool look effective.
Uses Repeat motif as panel on child or adult's ski sweater with matching scarf and mittens.

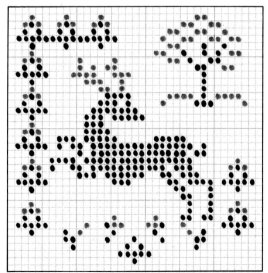

Repeat: 37 sts × 37 rows

Horse

Materials Medium-weight Shetland or acrylic yarn for sportswear; medium-weight cotton for summer tops.

Uses Single motif on child's pocket or pullover front, or adult's patchwork sweater.

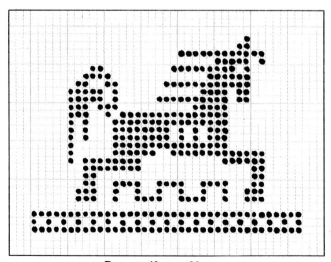

Repeat: 43 sts × 32 rows

Llama

Materials Medium-weight Shetland or acrylic yarn; mohair or alpaca for "fluffy" highlights.

Uses As repeat motif in traditional Peruvian pullovers, ponchos, scarves and hats; as border for long skirt.

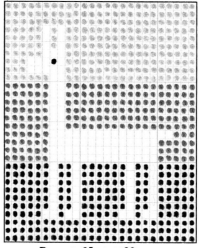

Repeat: 25 sts × 30 rows

Bird 1

Materials Medium-weight wool, cotton or acrylic yarn.
Uses Repeat motif as border for unisex V-neck, sleeveless pullover;
inset panel on ski wear; all-over pattern for dog's coat.

Repeat: 40 sts × 32 rows

Bird 2

Materials Medium-weight yarn of various composition – i.e. flecked or glitter mix, angora, Shetland or synthetics; heavy-weight cotton.
Uses Repeat pattern as border for evening skirt or jacket, tablecloth or tea towels; single motif on pot holders.

Repeat: 26 sts × 39 rows

93

Viking boat

Materials Double knitting yarn for winter warmth; medium-weight cotton or acrylic for easy care.

Uses Single motif for pencil case, pocket, rompers or bathing suit bottom.

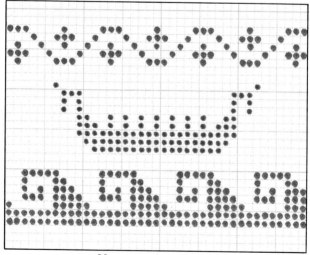

Non repeating pattern

Index

Acknowledgments

Samples
Mary Tebbs

Artist
Kuo Kang Chen

Photographer
Ian O'Leary

Typesetting
Text Processing Ltd.

Reproduction
F.E. Burman Ltd.